Hubert Clayton
Hubert Clayton
Hubert Clayton

Bardwell

HYGIENE AND HEALTH

Copyright Underwood & Underwood

Strike One! This young athlete has three things all boys and girls need—health, strength and skill

HYGIENE AND HEALTH SERIES

Hygiene and Health

BOOK ONE

By

CHARLES P. EMERSON

Dean and Professor of Medicine, Indiana University
School of Medicine

and

GEORGE HERBERT BETTS

Northwestern University
Evanston, Illinois

ILLUSTRATED

INDIANAPOLIS
THE BOBBS-MERRILL COMPANY
PUBLISHERS

Copyright, 1919, 1921, 1922, 1923,
By The Bobbs-Merrill Company

Printed in the United States of America

PRINTERS AND BINDERS

INTRODUCTION

The distinguishing feature of HYGIENE AND HEALTH is its outstanding aim and plan of causing the pupils *to form right habits of physical living*. In order to achieve this end, they must be led from day to day to *do* the things that lead to health and vigor, and to *avoid* the things that injure and weaken.

Each lesson therefore provides for certain suitable activities to be carried out. The children are asked to *learn by doing*, which is not only good pedagogy, but even better hygiene. The exercises provided are an integral part of the text, and are of the practical sort that find a setting in the daily life of every child. A skilful carrying out of the many simple experiments and projects given will not only bring zest and motive to the work, but will serve to carry the facts learned over into everyday practise. The wise teacher will, therefore, bend every effort to make the lessons *take hold* from day to day as they are taught. She will measure her success by the extent to which the children *live better* physically, here and now, because of the lessons learned, and by the extent to which they are forming *right hygienic habits* as they are passing through the text.

Those familiar with the texts in this field will note the avoidance in the present volume of two extremes: *first*, the over-emphasis on physiology and anatomy which characterizes the older type of text; and, *second*, the equally dangerous method of certain more recent texts, which offer a collection of mere stories and illustrations combined with sets of hygienic rules. This book stresses hygienic practise above all else, but does not fail to give the underlying facts and explanations for which the child's mind is at this stage ready, and which his curiosity demands. While immediate habits of right living are the great aim sought, the pupil is, step by step, led to an intelligent understanding of his own body and the laws which govern its welfare. The authors offer this volume as one small contribution to the present national movement to build up a better physical basis of life for our nation.

The material in Chapter XXXI, on Good Health Games at end of book, should be used throughout the school term.

THE AUTHORS.

ACKNOWLEDGMENTS

Grateful acknowledgments are made to the following organizations for permission to use photographs supplied by them: the National Tuberculosis Association, for pictures appearing on pages 5, 7, 23, 25, 26, 28, 30, 111, 123; the Massachusetts Association for the Prevention of Tuberculosis, for pictures appearing on pages 17, 43, 52, 97, 98; the National Girl Scouts, for the picture appearing on page 50; the Committee on Public Information, for the picture appearing on page 110; the Indiana State Board of Health, for the picture appearing on page 80, and the Boston Public Schools for the pictures appearing on pages 134 and 136.

THE AUTHORS.

CONTENTS

CHAPTER		PAGE
I	Making Our Habits Our Friends	1
II	Ready for "Inspection"	8
III	Health, Size and Growth	16
IV	Health Crusaders	22
V	The Body's Need of Food	32
VI	What We Eat	41
VII	Planning Our Meals	49
VIII	Learning to Eat	59
IX	Good and Bad Microbes	65
X	Protecting Our Food from Microbes	72
XI	Why We Should Get Rid of Flies	77
XII	Protection against Mosquitoes	83
XIII	The Air and Breathing	88
XIV	Living in Good Air	95
XV	The Heart and Its Work	104
XVI	Keeping the Body Straight	109
XVII	The Skin and Its Uses	116
XVIII	Keeping Clean	122
XIX	Clothing and Its Care	127
XX	When We Play	133
XXI	Sleep, Rest and Dreams	139
XXII	The Teeth	144
XXIII	How to Have Good Teeth	149
XXIV	Care of the Hair	155
XXV	Keeping the Nails in Order	161
XXVI	How to Have Good Eyes	167
XXVII	Care of the Ears	174
XXVIII	Better Not—Tobacco	180
XXIX	Better Not—Alcohol	184
XXX	When Accidents Happen	187
XXXI	Good Health Games	196
	Index	208

RULES OF THE HEALTH GAME

1. A full bath more than once a week.
2. Brushing the teeth at least once every day.
3. Sleeping long hours with windows open.
4. Drinking as much milk as possible, but no coffee or tea.
5. Eating some vegetables or fruit every day.
6. Drinking at least four glasses of water a day.
7. Playing part of every day out-of-doors.
8. A bowel movement every day.

HYGIENE AND HEALTH

CHAPTER I

MAKING OUR HABITS OUR FRIENDS

Did you ever notice which shoe you put on first in the morning? Or which arm you first put into your coat? Not that it matters which comes first in either case, but it is likely that you *do* put on your shoes and your coat in the same way every time.

This is because you have formed the habit of doing these things in a certain manner. Acts that we come to do without stopping to think about them, or without intending to do them we call our *habits*.

How habits are formed.—My friend Tom has a chum who stammers. Tom was thoughtless and unkind enough to mimic his chum several times. He did it in fun, of course, and had no notion of learning to stammer himself. But it was not long until Tom's mother noticed that he was stammering. When she spoke to him about it, Tom said he didn't mean to do it, and that it "just did itself." That was true. After he had performed the act of stammering a few times it went on and did itself without Tom intending it.

The habit was formed, and Tom is having much trouble in breaking it.

We can form either good habits or bad habits. If we perform only the right kind of acts our habits will be good. If we do things that ought not to be done and continue doing them for a little time we will have habits that are bad. For day by day our habits are growing out of our acts.

"Friend-habits" and "enemy-habits." — Dr. William James tells us that the great thing is to make our habits our friends instead of our enemies. Horace Mann once said, "Habit is a cable; we weave a thread of it each day and it becomes so strong we can not break it."

The real purpose of your studying physiology and hygiene is to help you form right habits of living. The way we care for our bodies to-day, to-morrow and the days that lie ahead quickly becomes habit; and our good health is after all largely the result of good habits.

Signs of good and bad habits.—I can explain what I mean in this way: If I should go about your school and examine the teeth of the boys and girls I should find that some have white, clean and attractive teeth. Their teeth are not discolored, they do not have holes in them, nor do they ache. I am quite sure that those who have teeth of this kind are the ones who have formed the habit of washing their teeth and keeping their mouths clean.

MAKING OUR HABITS OUR FRIENDS

It is probable that I should also find some with teeth that are not very clean nor attractive. Particles of food are lodged between the teeth, many of them have cavities, and some ache quite frequently. Is it not likely that the boys and girls who have teeth of this undesirable kind are the ones who have not formed the habit of caring for their teeth regularly?

The fine looking soldiers who stand so straight, look so spick and span, and carry themselves so well must pass "inspection" every morning. When the officer comes along every button and buckle must be in place, every uniform spotless, every shoe shined, and everything about each soldier neat, clean and in order. Soldiers quickly form these habits. It is a part of their training.

Looking after our habits.—Many schools are coming to have morning "inspection" like the soldiers. Suppose we should have inspection in your school room this morning. I am sure I should find some boys and girls whose hands and nails are clean and well-kept, whose hair shows care, and whose clothes are neat. They could pass "inspection"; they have formed right habits about these things.

Is it not possible that I should also find others with hands and nails that show less care, with hair that looks stubborn and untrained, and with clothes that need brushing or mending?

The difference is one of habits. If we have formed

HYGIENE AND HEALTH

the habit of cleaning our teeth and nails and of brushing our hair, so that we would no more think of starting our day without doing these things than we would of going without our meals or our sleep, then we may be sure that we can pass "inspection." Let us not forget that anybody who sees us can tell the kind of personal habits we have formed by noticing how we keep our hair, nails, teeth, shoes and clothes. These things always tell on us.

READY FOR INSPECTION

Clothes clean and neat, hair brushed, teeth and nails attended to, faces good-natured and smiling. "Friend-habits" forming

A good rule.—A very simple rule for habit forming is this: Anything that we want to keep on doing, as sleeping with open windows or sitting and walking straight, we should go at it and do until the habit is formed. Then the desirable act will go on of itself without care or effort.

MAKING OUR HABITS OUR FRIENDS

Anything that we do not want to keep on doing, as putting pencils in our mouths or eating too rapidly, we should be careful not to do at all because the habit will surely form in that direction. Things that we go on doing for a little time result in habits no matter whether we wish them to or not; they finally come to "do themselves."

All of us have many habits that are good and some that are bad. It is a good thing for each of us to make a list of the habits that he ought to form; also another list of the habits that he would like to break.

Habits to make our friends.— Some of the habits that we may make our friends are these:

EARLY TO BED

Twelve hours' sleep for young children, ten for all others. This is one of the best "friend-habits" we can form

> Opening our bedroom windows at night.
> Brushing the teeth after each meal.
> Sitting so that the light will not fall in the eyes when we read.
> Bathing several times a week.

HYGIENE AND HEALTH

Learning to say please, thank you, beg pardon, and other kindly expressions.

Being on time.

Going to bed and getting up at regular hours.

Keeping clothing, shoes, hair and nails neat.

Eating slowly and learning to like different kinds of foods.

Keeping good-natured and happy.

Habits to shun.—These habits are always our enemies; if we have formed any such habits we should go about it at once to break them:

Sprawling bent forward over our desk when we study.

Sliding down in our seat with the body cramped.

Biting the finger-nails or picking at the nose.

Coughing or sneezing near other people.

Not speaking our words clearly and distinctly.

Keeping our desk or room in disorder.

Being sullen, sour, cross or easily angry.

Carelessness about errands or other duties.

Eating candy or having soda fountain treats between meals.

The use of tobacco or liquor in any form.

Now stop and think a minute. How many of the "friend-habits" can you honestly say you have formed? How many of the "enemy-habits" have you?

MAKING OUR HABITS OUR FRIENDS 7

No doubt you can think of still other habits that you would like to form, and some that you ought to break. Try writing down at least five of each kind.

A letter from the authors.—At the very beginning the authors wish to give a personal message to the boys and girls who study this text. Our message is this: We want you not only to learn the things the book tells you, but we want you to *do* them. When the lessons tell you how to keep your bodies well, how to make them grow, how to be strong, do not be satisfied until you have *put the lessons into practise*. Do the right things until they become habits; refuse to do the things that injure you, so that you may not form wrong habits. Break off your "enemy-habits" now; form many new "friend-habits" just as fast as you can.

UP SMILING

No loitering in dressing or chores. Another good "friend-habit"

2—June 23.

CHAPTER II

READY FOR "INSPECTION"

Whether we have daily "inspection" in school or not we are, nevertheless, "inspected" every day by other people. Our classmates, our teachers, the visitors who call at our home, the people who notice us on the street— all these observe whether we are neat and clean and attractive.

We come to be known by the habits we form.— Just now, for example, without even glancing around the school room you know that there are certain ones of your friends who are pleasant to look upon, because they have clean clothes, clean bodies and neat appearance. You know this about them because they always *are* that way, and you know what to expect of them. Their "friend-habits" make them ready for "inspection" at any time.

On the other hand, it is just possible that, also without glancing around the room, you know that there are certain ones of your schoolmates who lack neatness, who are not so clean, and who are therefore not so attractive as the others. You know this about them without wait-

READY FOR "INSPECTION"

ing to look at them because they usually *are* this way. They have not formed the right "friend-habits," but have allowed "enemy-habits" to creep in.

Preparing for "inspection."—Of course one should be neat and clean and tidy just because one is ashamed *for one's own self* to be any other way. Boys and girls who really *care* about being clean would feel uncomfortable and ashamed to have unbrushed teeth or bodies that had missed a bath or clothes that had been neglected *even if no one else knew about it.*

No danger from bad air in this outdoor school

Besides wishing to be clean for our own sake, however, it is right that we should think about the impression we are constantly making on others by our appearance. Possibly your school is one of the many in which the first ten minutes of each morning is given to health and hygiene inspection. If so here are some of the things that will be done and the points that will be observed:

Class inspection.—When school has been called and the pupils are in their seats with coats, sweaters and rubbers removed the teacher will stand in front and give the signal, *"Attention!"* Every boy and girl sits erect, with head well up, feet flat on the floor and hands clasped, resting on the desk.

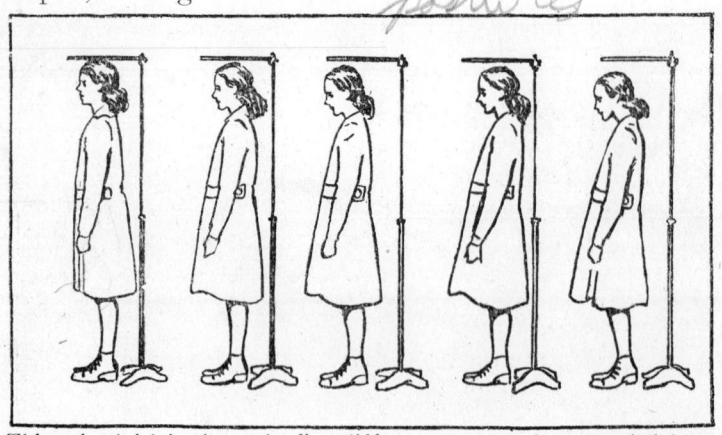

This schoolgirl is shown in five different postures from good (1) to very bad (5). Note how much taller she is when standing correctly

Clothing.—The teacher will then look down each line of seats to notice such things as these: Are the *blouses, shirts, dresses* and *collars* all neat, clean and in order? Are there buttons off or hanging loose? Are there torn or worn places that should have been mended?

READY FOR "INSPECTION"   11

Are there soiled spots that should have been sponged or washed? These points will tell whether one takes pride in his clothes or is careless. They will tell whether one is forming "friend-habits" or "enemy-habits."

Ties, ribbons, hair.—Next, the teacher will observe for the *ties,* the *hair ribbons* and the order of the *hair.* Sometimes the ties and ribbons are badly wrinkled and need pressing; sometimes they are tied carelessly and are crooked; sometimes they do not even look very fresh and require cleaning. It may also sometimes happen that some one's hair may have had only a "lick and a promise" instead of real brushing such as will make it stay in order.

Handkerchiefs.—Perhaps the teacher will ask all those who have brought fresh clean *handkerchiefs* to stand. This ought to include everybody, for even if one's nose is not unruly from a cold, one is likely to have to sneeze or cough. And of course one should never sneeze or cough without covering the nose and mouth with his handkerchief.

Tooth-brushes.—Those may next be asked to stand who have an individual *tooth-brush;* and then those to remain standing who have that morning brushed their teeth before coming to school. Surely those who can not truthfully say that they have a tooth-brush and that they faithfully use it will want to form this "friend-habit" immediately.

The feet.—The *shoes and stockings* may come in for observation next. Row after row may be asked to stand while the teacher notes whether the shoes are clean, laces not broken, stockings whole. For even our feet tell the story of our care or neglect in forming right habits.

Individual inspection.—It is possible that besides the class inspection your school may have *individual*

"Play while you play, but when you work do not play at all"

inspection. In this case the teacher will look more closely concerning each boy and girl.

READY FOR "INSPECTION"

Hands and arms.—The signal, *"Attention!"* is given; sleeves are rolled up to the elbows; hands and arms are placed on the desk top, palms down. Are your hands and wrists clean? Are your finger-nails properly trimmed, and are they clean? Do your nails show biting and tearing? Are there any cuts, bruises or sores that are not having proper treatment? Is there any rash, or breaking out, that needs attention? What stories a pair of hands can tell on their owner!

The teeth.—Teeth that are regularly well cleaned are shiny and white. To have your teeth inspected, draw your lips well apart so that they may be easily seen. It is well to remember that even if the school does not have daily "inspection" our teeth are observed by every one who cares to look, whenever we laugh or smile or speak. Well kept even teeth are beautiful and attractive.

Head and neck.—Of course every one washes his face before coming to school. Yet sometimes inspection shows that some spots have been missed. Did you ever sit behind a person and notice that the back of his neck was dirty? Or that he had failed to wash behind his ears! Or that you could see dirt and grime and dandruff sticking to the scalp!

So when you are sure that you are *clean* you will be proud to bend your head forward when the teacher comes by for inspection and *prove* that your "friend-habits" are on the job. You will be glad to have your hair and scalp examined because you know they are clean and fresh and that you can be proud of them instead of ashamed.

Interesting things to do.—1. Whether your school has "inspection" or not, "inspect" yourself when you are ready for school to make sure you are ready for "inspection" by your schoolmates and others.

2. Go to your mother or father when you are ready for school and offer yourself for "inspection" on the points mentioned in this chapter.

3. As you think the matter over, try to decide what points you need to be most careful about in order that you may be ready for "inspection" at any time.

4. As you think over a list of your friends are there some "enemy-habits" which make them less attractive than they would be without them?

5. Now try to determine whether you yourself have some "enemy-habits" which your friends or family would like to have you cure.

Health Problems

1. Tom wanted his hair to look well for morning school inspection, so he wet it and gave it two or three strokes with the brush. By the time he got to school his hair looked bristly

READY FOR "INSPECTION"

and stiff and stuck straight out instead of lying down on his head. How could Tom make his hair less unruly?

2. A certain boy came to school for a week with a large three-cornered tear in his coat sleeve. What would you recommend?
3. Hilda's teeth are of good shape but they are discolored and do not look clean. When it comes time for inspection she tries not to open her lips wide. What "friend-habit" do you think Hilda must lack?
4. Jack has a handkerchief, but it is rolled up in a tight ball and so soiled one can hardly tell its original color. A few moments ago Jack sneezed just back of where Mary was sitting, and he did not cover his nose and mouth with his handkerchief. Perhaps he was ashamed to show his handkerchief!
5. When the teacher asked those who had an individual tooth-brush to stand, nearly every one stood up. When she asked that only those who had brushed their teeth that morning should remain standing nearly a dozen sat down. The question is, What is the use of having a tooth-brush if one doesn't use it?

CHAPTER III

HEALTH, SIZE AND GROWTH

Nearly every one can tell how big he is—how many pounds he weighs and how many inches he is tall. But how many of you can tell how big you *ought* to be at your particular age?

When the baby is born it usually weighs about seven or eight pounds. If the baby is well it grows so fast that it has doubled its weight in six months and trebled its weight by its first birthday. So the baby weighs twenty or twenty-five pounds when it is a year old.

What our size ought to be.—But growth does not keep on at this rapid rate, and it is well it does not, for we should soon become too large to move about. When you entered school at the age of six you probably weighed forty or forty-five pounds, and your height should have been about forty-three or forty-four inches.

One of the things that each of us wants to know is whether our growth is keeping up. No one wants to be puny and undersized. We all desire to be as large and strong as others of our age.

Should we find out that our size is less than it ought

HEALTH, SIZE AND GROWTH

to be, we shall naturally wish to find out the cause, and if possible remedy it. If, on the other hand, we are up to standard, we shall try to avoid doing anything that might hinder our growth or lessen our strength. We should take pride in strong, well-built bodies.

Our size at different ages.— The school boys and girls of several large cities have been carefully measured and weighed, so that we are able to tell the size of American school children of various ages. You are to understand that the figures given are *averages*, some children being larger and some smaller.

Gaining weight every day, and proud of the fact.

For example, girls of ten years (to nearest birthday) run all the way from 47 to 59 inches in height; boys of ten years run all the way from 47 to 60 inches in height. In weight, girls of ten years vary all the way from 53 to 89 pounds; and boys from 54 to 91 pounds. The *average* height for girls of ten is 53 inches; for boys of ten about 54 inches. The *average* weight for girls of ten is 68 pounds; for boys of ten about 70 pounds.

Even more important than your exact height or weight is the *proportion* between your height and weight, and whether or not you are gaining steadily.

HYGIENE AND HEALTH

Right Height and Weight for Girls*

If your height is inches	8 yrs.	9 yrs.	10 yrs.	11 yrs.	12 yrs.
42	43				
43	44				
44	46				
45	48	49			
46	50	51			
47	51	52	53		
48	53	54	55	56	
49	55	56	57	58	
50	57	58	59	60	61
51	60	61	62	63	64
52	63	64	65	66	67
53	66	67	68	68	69
54	68	69	70	71	72
55		72	73	74	75
56		76	77	78	79
57			81	82	83
58			85	86	87
59			89	90	91
60				94	95
61				99	101
62				104	106
63				109	111
64					115
65					117
66					119

Right Height and Weight for Boys†

If your height is inches	8 yrs	9 yrs.	10 yrs.	11 yrs.	12 yrs.
42	44				
43	46				
44	47				
45	48	49			
46	50	51			
47	52	53	54		
48	55	55	56	57	
49	57	58	58	59	
50	59	60	60	61	62
51	61	62	63	64	65
52	63	64	65	67	68
53	66	67	68	69	70
54	69	70	71	72	73
55		73	74	75	76
56		77	78	79	80
57			81	82	83
58			84	85	86
59			87	88	89
60			91	92	93
61				95	97
62				100	102
63				105	107
64					113

Girls from *eight to eleven* years of age should gain about *eight ounces* each month; from *eleven to fourteen* years of age they should gain about *twelve ounces* a month.

---

*Weight and measures should be taken without shoes and in **usual indoor clothes**.

†A chart for keeping monthly height and weight records for your school for one year may be obtained for a few cents from the Child Health Organization of America, 370 Seventh Ave., New York, by whose courtesy these tables are published.

HEALTH, SIZE AND GROWTH

Boys from *eight to twelve* years of age should gain about *eight ounces* each month; boys from *twelve to sixteen* years should gain about *sixteen ounces* a month.

These tables of figures are not given for you to learn them, but that you may compare your own height and weight with the standard for your age. Your weight should be taken on good scales, and you should be in your indoor clothing. Your height should be taken without your shoes, when you are standing straight against the wall or on a measuring machine.

Two things that affect your size. —Whether you are large or small for your age will depend largely on two things: *First,* whether your parents, grandparents, and great-grandparents were naturally large or small of stature; *second,* whether you have kept well, received good care and had plenty of good food to keep you growing.

Taking his height on a measuring machine. Be sure to stand straight when your height is measured

Your *heredity,* or the tendency to size and growth given you by your parents and grandparents, you can not help nor hinder. But you can do much toward keeping well, eating the right foods, and thus giving nature a chance to bring you to your full size and strength.

Finding out about our family.—Now, after inquiring of your father and mother about the size of the members of their families, write down the answers to the following questions:

1. What is the weight of your father? His height?
2. What is the weight of your mother? Her height?
3. The weight of each of your grandparents? Their height?
4. Is your weight greater or less than the average for your age, and how much?
5. Is your height greater or less than the average for your age, and how much?

Health Problems

1. The boys and girls of the countries that were recently at war in Europe were nearly all found to be underweight. Can you tell why they were underweight?
2. The boys and girls who are being treated in children's hospitals, average less in size than those of the same age in school. Can you tell why?
3. It has been found that when milk is selling at a very high price many babies and young children, especially in the poorer

HEALTH, SIZE AND GROWTH

section of cities, show more sickness and do not grow so well. Why is this?

4. If you are larger or if you are smaller than the average for your age, how do you account for it?
5. It was found that during the European War the children took diseases more readily than in ordinary times. Can you account for this?
6. One of the chief things in treating a person for tuberculosis is to make sure that he has plenty of nourishing food. Is this also a safeguard against taking tuberculosis?
7. Bad complexion and pimples on the face are sometimes caused by wrong diet. What rules can you give for one who wants a good complexion?

Interesting things to do.—1. Take your weight carefully and discover whether it is greater or less than the *average* for your age (to nearest birthday).

2. Measure your height and discover whether it is greater or less than the *average* for your age.
3. Compare with the table and discover whether the proportion of your weight to your height is what it should be. If you are as much as *ten per cent.* under the average for your age and height you should give special attention to building up for you are *under weight*. If you are *twenty per cent.* over the average, you are *over weight* and your food and exercise may need to be modified. In either case it would be well to consult a physician.

CHAPTER IV

HEALTH CRUSADERS

We never miss the water till the well runs dry, says the old adage. In like manner we never know the value of health until we are ill.

There are at any one time about three million people sick in the United States. This is three persons out of every one hundred. If you live in a town of one thousand inhabitants, there are about thirty of your neighbors sick to-day and under the doctor's care.

Why we should keep well.—Sickness brings sorrow, worry and trouble. It checks the growth of the young. It wastes time and money. The cost in the United States of unnecessary sickness, or sickness that could have been prevented, is estimated at a billion dollars a year. This is nearly twice as much money as is spent on our schools.

At times sickness may come upon us through no fault of our own. But many of our aches and pains are the result of our own carelessness or lack of knowledge.

Planning for good health.—The other day a boy I know went skating. He is a fine skater, but there

HEALTH CRUSADERS

was water on the ice and he got his feet wet. Instead of changing his shoes and stockings when he came home, he sat through the evening with his feet damp. He is now down with a severe cold, and the doctor fears pneumonia. And all because Harry had not formed the habit of attending to wet feet the moment he came into the house!

RECESS

Play hard. Put nothing dirty in your mouth

Have you ever eaten something you knew you ought not to eat, and then found yourself ill because of it? Have you never had toothache from a decayed tooth which had been neglected? It is even possible that your weight and height are less now than they should be on account of some sickness which a little care might have prevented.

Things to be proud of.—The girls and boys who read this book should be well. They should plan for good health. They should be strong, and not easily tired. They should grow fast, and be free from aches and pains. They should not take cold easily, nor be subject to headaches, earaches, toothaches. They should be hungry for every meal, and enjoy their food. They should not easily take contagious diseases to which they may be exposed. They should have the habit of being healthy and happy!

A young friend of mine in the sixth grade boasts that he has not lost a day from school since he entered the first grade. This means that he has kept well. He has not had to have the doctor called to see him in all that time. I think he has a right to be proud of his record. He has a right to be proud of his good health. And of course he is sturdy and strong and of good size. This is his reward for keeping well.

Questions worth answering.—The lessons of this book are to tell you how to keep well, and how to grow large and strong. They will show you how to prevent sickness, and how to save the pain and trouble it brings. Let us now stop a moment and answer the following questions in order to see what lessons we most need to learn.

1. How many times have you been so ill during the past year that you had to take medicine?
2. How many times have you had to stay in bed on account of sickness?

HEALTH CRUSADERS

3. How many times have you had to have the doctor?
4. How much time have you lost from school or from work or from play because of being ill?
5. How much did your medicine and the doctor cost?
6. Have you had any pains, aches, sore throat, colds, or other troubles which have not been bad enough that you had to take medicine or stay out of school?

Now, after answering these questions, see whether, in any sickness you may have had, you can tell what brought on the trouble. If a cold, how did you happen to take it; if indigestion, what caused it, and so on. Can you suggest what you might have done to avoid being ill? Who or what was to blame?

Modern Health Crusaders.*—You no doubt know stories of the old Crusaders who fought for every good cause and did so many brave deeds that we honor them to this day. These crusaders were of different ranks, de-

Pennant of the Modern Health Crusaders

pending on how much good they had done and how many battles they had won. First, the crusader was given the rank of Page; if he did well he was

---
*Both plan and matter are borrowed from published material of the National Tuberculosis Association.

next made a Squire; and finally he might rise to the rank of Knight. To become a Knight was a very high honor.

There is to-day a new kind of crusaders, the "Modern Health Crusaders." The Modern Health Crusaders is an organization started by the National Tuberculosis Association. It already has many members. Every boy and girl who reads this book may become a member and win honors like the crusaders of old. The different ranks that you can win are: *first*, Page; *second*, Squire; *third*, Knight; *fourth*, Knight Banneret.

The way one wins honors as a Modern Health Crusader is by doing faithfully a certain number of "health chores" each week. Seventy-two chores done in one week make a perfect score. Here is a daily statement of the chores:

Squire's Button of the Modern Health Crusaders

Knight's Pin of Modern Health Crusaders

1. I washed my hands before each meal to-day.
2. I washed not only my face, but my ears and neck and I cleaned my finger-nails to-day.
3. I tried to-day to keep fingers, pencils and everything that might be unclean out of my mouth and nose.

HEALTH CRUSADERS

4. I drank a glass of water before each meal and before going to bed, and drank no tea, coffee nor other injurious drinks to-day.

5. I brushed my teeth thoroughly in the morning and in the evening to-day.

6. I took ten or more slow, deep breaths of fresh air to-day.

7. I played outdoors or with windows open more than thirty minutes to-day.

8. I was in bed ten* hours or more last night and kept my window open.

9. I tried to-day to sit up and stand straight, to eat slowly, and to attend to toilet and each need of my body at its *regular* time.

10. I tried to-day to keep neat and cheerful constantly and to be helpful to others.

11. I took a full bath on each of two days of the week.

How to win the different ranks.—In order to do all seventy-two chores in one week requires that you shall do each of the first ten chores daily, and take a full bath on each of two days of the week. This is what you are required to do for each of the different titles:

---

*Boys and girls thirteen years of age may change this to "nine hours." Those under nine years should sleep eleven hours at least.

28 HYGIENE AND HEALTH

To be a Page, at least 54 chores in each of two weeks.

To be a Squire, at least 54 chores for a total of five weeks.

To be a Knight, at least 54 chores for a total of ten weeks.

To be a Knight Banneret, at least 54 chores for a total of fifteen weeks.

The record of health chores must be carefully kept on a blank like the one which follows. When you have done enough chores for a title, take the record properly filled to your teacher for her to approve. She must be satisfied with your cleanness from day to day, and know that you are doing your chores faithfully.

Rules for a "Crusader"—Fresh air, study hard, sit up straight at your desk

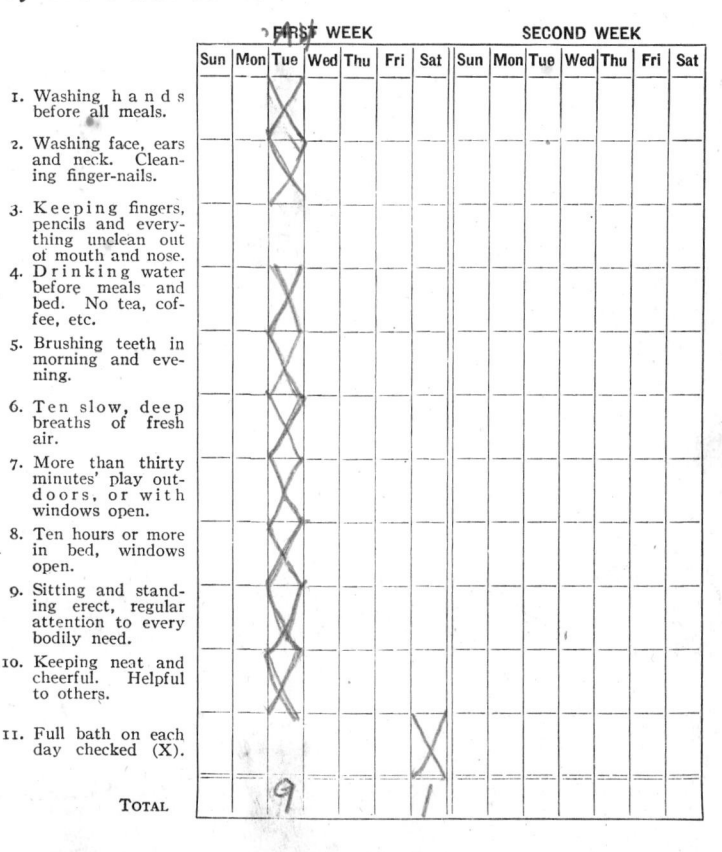

HEALTH CRUSADERS 29

Health Chore Record Blank.—Check X for each day chore was done:

	FIRST WEEK							SECOND WEEK						
	Sun	Mon	Tue	Wed	Thu	Fri	Sat	Sun	Mon	Tue	Wed	Thu	Fri	Sat
1. Washing hands before all meals.			X											
2. Washing face, ears and neck. Cleaning finger-nails.			X											
3. Keeping fingers, pencils and everything unclean out of mouth and nose.														
4. Drinking water before meals and bed. No tea, coffee, etc.			X											
5. Brushing teeth in morning and evening.			X											
6. Ten slow, deep breaths of fresh air.														
7. More than thirty minutes' play outdoors, or with windows open.			X											
8. Ten hours or more in bed, windows open.			X											
9. Sitting and standing erect, regular attention to every bodily need.			X											
10. Keeping neat and cheerful. Helpful to others.														
11. Full bath on each day checked (X).						X								
TOTAL			9											

Note to the teacher: The authors strongly urge that not only the class using this text, but the entire school, be organized into a band of Modern Health Crusaders. Many schools are using this plan to establish habits of hygienic living. The scope of the organization is national. A letter addressed to the National Tuberculosis Association, New York, or to your state Junior Red Cross will bring you full information and samples of blanks, etc.

HYGIENE AND HEALTH

Interesting things to do.—Some helpful things which members of the Modern Health Crusaders might do are the following; still others may be suggested by the teacher:

The "Crusader" has formed "friend-habits" like these—Glass of water, brush teeth, a hot bath twice a week

1. Taking charge, under the teacher's directions, of the opening of windows for the ventilation of the school room.
2. Flushing the room with all doors and windows open at recess.
3. Helping conduct morning "inspection."
4. Keeping room, halls, toilets and school yard clear of rubbish.
5. Observing whether laws governing cleanliness are obeyed in markets
6. Joining an anti-spitting, anti-coughing and anti-sneezing crusade.
7. Learning to make and apply bandages for cuts, sprains and bruises.

HEALTH CRUSADERS

8. Learning to choose the proper food and neatly pack school and picnic lunches.
9. Assisting in "tooth-brush drill."
10. Demonstrating how to treat burns, frost-bites, etc.

Health Problems

1. Report on Health Chores.
2. There are several million Health Crusaders among the school boys and girls of this country—will you be one?
3. Which of the eleven health chores do you find it hardest to remember or do? If you form the habit of doing this thing then it will be easy—it will "do itself."
4. How does one go about it to form a habit? How does one go about it to break a habit he wishes to be rid of?
5. I saw a boy holding a pencil in his mouth the other day. He put the pencil in his pocket and soon Ned came and borrowed it to write with. After a few minutes Ned had the pencil in *his* mouth. Besides the dirtiness of it, how many boys were in danger of taking disease?
6. Suppose every boy and girl in the United States should turn Health Crusader and do all the health chores regularly. Do you think they would grow larger and stronger? What would be the effect on the doctors' income?
7. Do you think people like boys and girls better when they are clean, well and wholesome?

CHAPTER V

THE BODY'S NEED OF FOOD

If I should ask you why we need to eat, I suppose the most natural answer would be because we get hungry.

This seems reason enough. Yet there are even more important reasons than this. *Hunger is nature's way of telling us that the body needs food.* And without hunger to remind us I fear that we should often neglect to give the body the food it requires.

Why the body needs food.—There are two great reasons why the body must have food: *First*, to replace the worn-out tissues of our muscles, bones, nerves, etc., and add new material for our growth. *Second*, to supply the energy needed by the body to do its work and keep up its heat.

Does it seem strange that we should speak of the body wearing out? Yet every tissue of your body, its muscles, bones, nerves, and all other parts, is constantly wearing away just as surely as your clothes wear out.

Not a movement you make, not an errand you run, not a game you play but thousands upon thousands of

THE BODY'S NEED OF FOOD

the tiny cells or particles which make up the tissues of your body work harder and so need more food, and wear out faster and so need new material with which to repair themselves. Even the thinking you do in learning this lesson means more work by the brain cells just as truly as your running means more work by the muscle cells of your leg. But you might say then why not rest always? Why not save all these cells this wear and tear? No, a living cell like a healthy boy was made to work. It gets strong and skilful by working, and grows stronger the more it works. If you let it rest too much it will first sicken and then may die. The important lesson for us to learn is not to tire the cells too much and to give them plenty of food and ample time to rest and repair themselves.

Replacing worn-out tissues.—Now it is clear that these worn-out tissues must be replaced, or the body would soon all waste away. Our bodies are much like the jack-knife which a man was proud of having carried for twenty-five years. The knife had had one new handle and several new blades during that time, but the owner still considered it the same old knife.

We think of keeping the same bodies from year to year, yet the old tissues are constantly being removed and new tissues built in. The result is that we have almost completely new bodies every few years.

34 HYGIENE AND HEALTH

Building new tissues. — We must also *grow*. You have already seen how the baby increases its

FROM THIS   TO THIS
In a year. The increase all came from the food which the baby ate

weight threefold the first year, and how each of us continues to add to his size from year to year until he

THE BODY'S NEED OF FOOD

has reached his full stature.

All the material for the repairing of worn-out tissues and the adding of new must come from our food. What you eat to-day will in a few hours become a part of your body. The potatoes, the bread, the meat, the milk, will become muscle, blood, brain, and other tissues.

Supplying energy.—Besides its supply of new tissue, the body must also be supplied with force or *energy*. It requires energy to work, or play, or think. It requires energy just to *be alive*, even. It requires energy also to keep up the heat of the body.

The food which this young athlete eats must not only make him grow, but must also supply the *energy* which he constantly uses

Yesterday I stood by the railway track and watched a long train sweep by. It was drawn by a monster locomotive, and was going sixty miles an hour. I thought what an amount of power, what energy! As I turned from the train, I saw two boys coming down the road at a fast pace. They were running a race. They flashed past me, and I said, "Here is power, here is energy too."

And so it was. It was energy or force which drove both the engine and the boys. The energy which had been stored up in the coal ages ago was set free by burning the coal, and the engine used the power to pull the train.

Likewise, the energy which had been stored up in the food eaten by the boys was set free by burning the food in their bodies. It was this that had given them the power and endurance used in their race. Just as the locomotive is without power until it gets the energy of the coal, so the body is without strength until it receives the energy from its food.

Furnishing heat.—The body must also have its supply of *heat*. I do not mean now the heat that comes from our fires or from the sun, but the heat that comes from within the body itself. We try to keep the temperature of our rooms near 70 degrees. When we are well the temperature of our bodies is about 99 degrees. The body keeps this temperature even when we are out-of-doors in the extreme cold.

Just as we heat our houses with the coal we feed the furnace, so we heat our bodies with the food we eat.

THE BODY'S NEED OF FOOD

A part of our food is slowly burned up in the tissues of the body where, instead of producing a red-hot fire like that in our furnace, it makes heat enough to keep the temperature of the body up to nearly 99 degrees.

What an amazing thought—thousands, yes millions, of tiny fires burning throughout our bodies, but so well

It is sometimes as much fun to work as it is to play

controlled that they never get too hot nor too cold as long as we keep well and have proper food!

When we lack food.—When people do not have food enough, they come to have a starved look. They grow thin and spindling and pale. Their bodies are being worn away faster than they are built up.

Lack of food also reduces the body's energy, so that the strength fails. The poor food that many European people were obliged to live on before the end of the great war so weakened them that they were not able to do more than half of the work expected of them. We are always careful to feed our soldiers, workmen and athletes well, so that they may be at their best in strength.

One who is poorly fed is unable to withstand severe cold. Explorers in the arctic regions have found that they do not greatly mind the very cold weather as long as they have plenty of good food. But when the food supply runs low, they are easily chilled by the cold. Their bodies are then without fuel to burn.

This all means, then, that if we would grow fast, if we would appear plump and well-fed instead of thin and scrawny, we must have enough good food to eat. If we would have strength, energy and endurance for work and play, if we would be able to stand cold winters and stormy weather, we must give the body the food it requires.

Our food must be of the right kind.—In this favored land of ours there are very few who are obliged to go hungry. Yet even in America there are some who do not have sufficient food, or whose food is not of the kind they require. There are boys and girls who will never reach their full growth and be as large and strong as nature intended them to be simply because they do not have enough to eat.

Probably few of the boys and girls who read these

THE BODY'S NEED OF FOOD

words are so poor as to lack food. But there are other things to take into account besides having a sufficient quantity of food. The food must be of the *right kinds*, and it must be *properly prepared* and *properly eaten*. Our next lessons will deal with some of these questions.

Interesting things to do.—Think out and write down the answers to the following questions:

1. In certain New York and Chicago schools where an investigation was made it was found that about one boy or girl out of every twelve regularly came to school with no breakfast. How would you expect this to affect their size? Their strength? Their quickness to learn? Their power to withstand the winter cold?

2. One who has sufficient food of a kind that agrees with him and causes him to grow strong and sturdy is said to have *good nutrition;* one who does not have enough food, or one whose food fails to nourish him as it should, leaving him flabby, undersized, thin, pale, easily tired and unable to stand severe cold, is said to have *poor nutrition*. Would you say that your nutrition is good or poor? By what signs do you judge?

3. Another way to test your nutrition is as follows: With a tape line measure the girth of your arm around the largest part above the elbow (Do not bend the arm). Measure the girth of your chest

HYGIENE AND HEALTH

(Do not fill the lungs). Next, multiply your arm girth by 100; then divide this product by the girth of your chest. If the quotient is 30 or more it indicates good nutrition; if less than 30, poor nutrition. For example, a boy I know measures 8.5 inches around his arm and 28 inches around his chest. This is the way to figure his nutrition:

8.5 × 100 = 850

850 ÷ 28 = 30.4

This boy's nutrition is therefore about up to the average.

Facts that are worth remembering.—1. The material for your growth all comes from your food. There is no other place to get it. If you lack food material, or if ill health keeps you from digesting and using what you eat, your growth will be slow and you will probably be under size.

2. All your force, energy and endurance come from your food. They can never be better than your food supply.

3. The fuel for the body's heat is supplied by the food we eat, and a poor fuel supply for the body means imperfect heating there, just as lack of good coal would mean poor heating for our houses.

4. The only way to get growth, strength and health is from good food, well cooked and properly eaten.

CHAPTER VI

WHAT WE EAT

It would seem strange, would it not, for a person to starve to death while he had an abundance of food? Yet this would be possible if he were allowed but one single kind of food. If you should give me plenty of bread, for example, and nothing else, I should certainly finally die of starvation. The result would be the same if you gave me nothing but lean meat. One can not live on any one such food as bread or meat alone, necessary as both are in our diet.

The two kinds of food we need.—The reason for this becomes clear when we remember that the body must have both *tissue building* and *energy producing* foods. Now, not all foods are capable of serving both of these purposes. One would surely starve if he ate ever so much of a food that would build tissues, but would not produce energy; and he would starve just as readily if he were to eat the energy producers, but lacked the tissue builders.

None of us is in danger of actual starvation, of course, for we do not try to live on one single kind of food. Yet it is very necessary that we so choose our food that we shall have a "balanced ration." By a balanced ration is meant a variety of food so chosen as to supply the body with all the different food materials it requires.

What happens if we do not have a "balanced ration."—If we leave out of our diet the foods that are intended to build up new tissues, then we shall not grow as fast as we should, and may even lose in weight and strength.

If, on the other hand, our diet is short in the foods that supply energy, we shall be weak and lack ambition and endurance. In either case our health will not be good, and we shall be more liable to sickness and disease.

It is therefore possible, you see, that though all the boys and girls who study this book may have *enough* to eat, they may not always live on a properly balanced diet, and some of you may not be growing as fast as you should from lack of tissue builders in your diet. Others may not be able to run as fast, or lift as much, or learn as easily, or resist disease as well as they ought because they do not eat the *right kinds* of food.

There are some foods that contain almost every element that the body needs, and which should therefore form an important part of our diet.

The best foods.—Milk is one such food. The baby lives and thrives on milk alone. Milk continues to be one of our most necessary foods throughout our life.

WHAT WE EAT

Especially should boys and girls drink plenty of good milk. For milk contains materials both for tissue building and energy. Milk therefore favors rapid growth, and will make us strong and sturdy.

Eggs are also one of our best foods. Did you ever think that an egg contains within its shell everything

These young Americans will need more food-fuel during the winter than in the summer months

that finally goes to make up the body of the chick that hatches from it? The materials that are needed to make muscles, bones, brain, blood and every other tissue have all been provided in just the right proportions.

When we eat an egg we are therefore getting precisely the materials we need for our own tissues, instead of allowing them to grow into the tissues of a chicken.

Wheat bread an important food.—Bread made from wheat is so important a food that it is called the "staff of life." Whatever else we may have on our tables, we usually have plenty of bread. Yet it is only in recent times that it has been possible to raise enough wheat so that the common people could have it for their daily food.

And even yet there are many millions of people in India, China and some other parts of the world who have never tasted wheat bread. Instead of wheat, they eat rice, rye, corn or other grains. During the European war many Americans went without wheat that we might ship it to our allies.

Almost all the common cereals make excellent foods when eaten along with meats, milk, eggs, butter, sugar and the like. One of the best ways in which cereals can be prepared is in the form of gruel, porridge, or the prepared breakfast foods that come to us in packages.

Meat foods.—Meat is an excellent part of our diet, though it does not need to be eaten in large quantities. Once a day is often enough to eat meat. In fact three or four times a week is sufficient if we have eggs and milk.

Lean meat goes largely to the building up of our tissues for the growth and repair of the body. Fat meat is used chiefly in the production of the body's heat. The Eskimos eat large quantities of seal blubber, or fat, and this enables them to withstand the extreme cold of the far North.

WHAT WE EAT 45

Fruits and vegetables.—One should eat freely of the common fruits and vegetables. This is highly important for health and growth. An old saying is that "an apple a day keeps the doctor away." Fresh fruits and vegetables should be eaten daily when they are in season. Stored, canned or dried fruits and

Milk, bread, vegetables and fruits are necessary foods

vegetables should form a regular part of the daily ration during the winter. Hardly a meal, certainly not a day, should pass without our eating a liberal amount of this most necessary kind of food. Nearly all vegetables are good energy producers.

Sugar.—Everybody likes sugar and candy. These should form a part of our food, but not in too great quantities. During the great war many of our allies in Europe were suffering for want of sugar, and we were asked to send them what we could spare.

It would seem that we ought to be able to spare no small amount, for on the average each of us eats more than eighty pounds of sugar a year, either in sweetening our food and drink or making candy. About half this amount is all we really need as food. Sugar goes to the producing of energy. It does not build body tissues.

Water.—Nor must we forget water as an important part of our food. While water does not directly rebuild our tissues nor supply energy, it is highly necessary to the welfare of the body. Indeed, one can go without solid food much longer than he can without water. Men lost on the desert or adrift on the ocean without water to drink suffer cruelly, and even go insane from thirst.

The body's need for water does not seem strange when we know that about two-thirds of our weight is made up of the water in our tissues. This means that if you now weigh seventy-five pounds, the water in your muscles, bones, fat, blood, and other tissues weighs fully fifty pounds. The really solid part of you therefore weighs only about twenty-five pounds. No wonder that you need water as a part of your food!

We get a part of the water we require in the foods we eat, for most foods contain a large proportion of water. Potatoes, for example, are about seventy-five

WHAT WE EAT

per cent. water; meat is from sixty to eighty per cent. water; and milk nearly ninety per cent. water.

Yet we do not secure water enough in such ways, and must constantly drink a considerable amount. Many people do not drink enough water to keep them in the best of health and strength. Boys and girls from ten to twelve years of age should usually drink as much as three or four pints of *pure* water each day. Even though one does not feel thirsty he should, nevertheless, drink his full amount of water.

Interesting questions to answer.—1. Prisoners who disobey rules in the penitentiary are sometimes punished by being fed on bread and water. Bread is a good tissue builder, but not a good energy producer. How do you think this kind of diet will affect a man who lives on it for a number of weeks?

2. Butter and fat meat are heat producing foods. Would you expect the people who live in hot or in cold climates to care most for them? When do we care most for them, in summer or in winter?

3. We use up energy faster when we labor or play hard than when we are idle. We also use up energy faster when the weather is cold than when it is hot. When should you naturally get more hungry and eat more food, on days when you are not exercising much, or when you are active? In winter or in summer?

HYGIENE AND HEALTH

Facts to be remembered.—The important lessons which we should remember from this chapter might be stated as follows:

> We should not live on too narrow a range of foods.
>
> Our diet should be simple. It should include all great groups of foods, such as milk and eggs, the cereal grains, vegetables, fruits, meats, sweets, and pure water.
>
> We must have both the tissue builders and energy producers. If we eat a varied diet we shall be sure to have both in abundance.

Health Problems

1. Report on Health Chores.
2. Make a list of all that you have had to eat and to drink in the last twenty-four hours. Have you eaten anything that does not "agree" with you? Have you had enough nourishing food? Have you had enough variety?
3. Jamie is rather hard to cook for. He complains that he "does not like vegetables." He rebels at oatmeal and cream, and wants coffee instead of milk to drink. Jamie is about ten pounds underweight. Can you guess why?
4. Jennie has noticed that, though she may feel rather tired and weak just before a meal, she feels strong and ready for play or work after she has eaten. Can you explain the reason?
5. Do you ever go to the table hungry and then not feel like eating much after you have started your meal? If so, what is the matter?

CHAPTER VII

PLANNING OUR MEALS

What shall we have for breakfast? What shall we have for dinner? What shall we have for supper? And, if we carry our lunch to school, what shall we take?

Perhaps you will say, "Whatever our mothers prepare for us." Or you may name the one thing you like best. Yet no doubt your mother would like you to be able to help plan for your meals; and you will, of course, want something besides the particular food you like best.

First of all, our meals should be *palatable;* we should like our food and enjoy eating it. This is not just for the pleasure we may get from our meals, though that is worth while. It is chiefly because our stomachs digest better and we get more good from food that we enjoy.

Why our food should be palatable.—You have noticed that your mouth "waters" when you see something you especially like to eat. But your mouth never waters for a dose of medicine or a dish of food that you dislike.

HYGIENE AND HEALTH

Now this watering of the mouth is caused by the *saliva*, which begins to flow at the thought or sight of pleasing food. A similar liquid called *gastric juice* begins to flow in the stomach whenever the saliva starts. And these are the two chief fluids that bring

The fun of outdoor cooking

about the digestion of our food. If they flow freely the food is properly digested. If they fail to flow, the digestion is hindered.

Why meal-time should be cheerful.—Pleasing and attractive surroundings as well as a palatable taste help us to enjoy our meals. A well set table, dishes of food well served and attractively arranged, pleasant conversation, laughter and cheer are good for the digestion.

PLANNING OUR MEALS

On the other hand, food that does not look attractive nor have a pleasing taste, or conversation that makes us gloomy or unhappy is sure to hinder digestion and take something from the value of the meal.

What an experiment on a dog showed.— A number of years ago several French physicians performed an interesting experiment on a dog. They cut in his neck a small slit through which they could force food into the dog's stomach without the dog eating it or even seeing the food.

They had a device fixed so they could watch what was taking place in the stomach. They found that food passed into the stomach through this cut would remain for several hours without digestion taking place. The gastric juice did not flow out and mix with the food.

They then brought more food to the dog and this time allowed him to see it and smell it. The dog wanted the food and his mouth watered for it, but they did not give him any. Immediately, however, the gastric juice began to flow in the stomach and digestion started upon the food that had remained undigested for several hours.

As soon as the dog wanted the food and had pleasant thoughts of eating, his stomach was ready to begin work. Eating and liking the food were good for the digestion.

HYGIENE AND HEALTH

Right and wrong kinds of breakfasts.—Breakfast is often a hurried and rather unsatisfactory meal. I have known boys and girls to get up late, snatch a few bites, and rush off to school without having time

Having a schoolroom lunch of milk and cookies. Paper cups are used and then destroyed, so that no one drinks out of a cup that has been used by another

to eat properly. School physicians in Boston and New York found that nearly one-half of the children had had an unsatisfactory breakfast. No wonder that many of them were thin and skinny!

Now what foods make a good breakfast? Dr. Earnest Hoag, who was studying children's dietaries among certain schools of Minnesota, discovered that

PLANNING OUR MEALS

eighty-five per cent. of the children had no fruit for breakfast. More than half of them had a breakfast that contained no tissue building foods. Such breakfasts are unsatisfactory. They are a poor start for the day!

How to plan our breakfasts.—Let us suppose that we are planning the breakfasts for the boys and girls of our class for a week. What shall we have? We shall want a variety, of course, and will not have just the same things every morning. But there are some *classes* of food that we will always have in some form.

Fruit, fresh if possible, such as baked apple, bananas, oranges, grapes, prunes, berries, or grapefruit. It is better that the fruit be eaten first.

Cereal and cream. Oat meal, cream of wheat, puffed rice, or any of the prepared breakfast foods are good.

Bread and butter. It is best to have the bread toasted crisp, at least for some of the days of the week. Warm bread should usually not be eaten. Take a piece of warm bread and mold it like a marble, and you will see how heavy and soggy it becomes.

Milk or cocoa. Boys and girls should drink milk or cocoa instead of coffee or tea, which are a stimulant rather than a food.

If we are to have meat for dinner we shall not need any for breakfast, providing we have sufficient foods of other kinds.

Breakfast plans for a week.—Now from the groups of foods just given plan your breakfasts for one week, showing just what you will serve each day. The following is a sample for one day's breakfast:

Sliced Orange

Oatmeal and Cream   Whole Wheat Muffins

Milk Flavored with Cocoa

How does the list of breakfasts you have planned compare with what you actually had for your breakfasts for the last week?

How to plan our dinners.—Now about our dinners, which may come either at noon or in the evening. When we have to go home some distance at noon for our dinners it is often hard not to be hurried. But, since dinner is our heaviest meal, it should be eaten slowly and with time to enjoy it. Dinner should have a larger variety of foods and also a larger quantity than breakfast. Meat and vegetables are an important part of the dinner. The following are groups of foods suitable for dinner:

Meats. Beef, broiled, baked or made into hamburg steak. Pork is not a good food for children. Fish, broiled or made into balls. Chicken, stewed or baked. Mutton, broiled or baked.

Vegetables. Potatoes boiled or baked, sweet potatoes, peas, beans, carrots, onions, tomatoes, cabbage, cauliflower, spinach, etc. At least one green leafy vegetable should be served at every dinner; two are better.

PLANNING OUR MEALS

Fruit, as apples or other fresh fruits, cranberry sauce, canned fruits.

Dessert. Puddings, such as rice, tapioca, Charlotte-russe, baked custard, ice-cream. Pies are not as good desserts, especially for children, as puddings.

A boys' garden club raises valuable food and has real enjoyment while doing it

Dinner plans for a week.—Plan the dinners which you would like for one week, making sure that you provide for such foods as will favor your growth and health. The following is a sample for one day's dinner:

  Roast beef with brown gravy Mashed potatoes
   Creamed peas Cranberry sauce
   Rice pudding with lemon sauce Milk

Now make a list of what you actually had for your dinners for the past week, and compare with your plan. What differences do you note?

Supper plans.—For supper or for luncheon, we may have much the same classes of foods as for breakfast and dinner, but they may be differently prepared. This will give variety and make them palatable.

Make a plan for your suppers for one week. The following is a sample for one day:

Creamed tomato soup
Whole wheat bread, with butter   One poached egg
Baked apple   Cake
Milk

How does the list you have made correspond with the suppers you usually have?

Planning the school lunch.—If we must carry our lunch to school, instead of having dinner at home, we should then have dinner in the evening. A school lunch should be neatly and attractively packed. Sandwiches, cake, cheese and other moist foods should be wrapped in paraffin paper to keep them fresh and clean. The following are samples of good school lunches:

Cup of baked beans   Jam sandwich
Egg sandwich   Plain bread and butter sandwich
Ginger cookies   Stuffed dates

PLANNING OUR MEALS 57

Hot potato soup (made at school)   One apple
Cup cottage cheese   Bread and butter
Two frosted cakes

Make a plan for your school lunches for one

Canning food prevents food waste and furnishes pleasant occupation for girls

week. Tell or show how you would prepare and pack each article so that it will keep well and look neat and attractive.

Foods that are not good for us.—There are some things used for food by many people that are not good, especially for growing children. These things we

HYGIENE AND HEALTH

should not make a regular part of our diet. Some such articles to be avoided are the following:

Hot bread or biscuits. They are hard to digest.

Griddle cakes for breakfast. Cereals are better.

All kinds of pie. Puddings, ice-cream and fruits are preferable.

Fried meats of every kind. Meats should be broiled or baked.

Fried potatoes, fried bread, fried mush or other fried foods.

Candy, except at meal-time, or too much of sweets at any time.

Ice-cream cones, sodas, or iced drinks at soda fountains between meals.

Health Problems

1. Report on Health Chores.
2. Mary and Grace were each given fifteen cents with which to buy their lunch at noon when they go to school. Mary bought hot soup, a baked potato, and a slice of bread and butter and a small dish of ice-cream. Grace bought ten cents' worth of candy and a sandwich. Who made the better bargain, and why?
3. Henry says he doesn't like cereal and cream or eggs for breakfast, but wants his mother to serve buckwheat cakes and sirup every morning. What do you think Henry's mother ought to do about it?
4. Elizabeth likes fudge and she usually eats several pieces when she comes home from school; then she is not hungry for supper. What would you recommend?

CHAPTER VIII

LEARNING TO EAT

Eating is so natural and easy that it seems strange to speak of learning to eat. Yet all of us have had to learn to eat.

To understand this, you need but to observe the baby in his first attempts to feed himself. He often makes a rather sorry mess of things, and we excuse him by saying he will learn better by and by.

Every one wants, of course, to be dainty and clean about his eating. For our manners and good breeding never stand out more plainly than when we are at the table. No one admires the greedy way in which pigs eat, nor would any one want it said of himself that "he eats like a pig." Well-bred people therefore learn to eat quietly, not making unnecessary noises as they chew or swallow their food.

Why we should eat slowly.—Besides not being good manners, there is another reason why we should not eat rapidly. It takes time to chew one's food and get it ready for swallowing. Food that is swallowed without proper chewing is not well mixed with the saliva. It comes to the stomach in coarse chunks.

The stomach then has to work much harder to digest it than if it had been well chewed. In fact, some of the coarser lumps may never be digested at all, and hence much of their food value is lost and they cause indigestion.

Chickens can gulp their food down, since they have gizzards. Chickens keep in their gizzards gravel, pieces of glass and other hard substances which help grind their food after it is swallowed. Since we do not have gizzards, we should not swallow our food without chewing, the way chickens do.

When we are tempted to eat too much.—There is sometimes a temptation to eat too much at one time. Some day we find that mother has prepared shortcake, dumplings, or some pudding that we especially like. We are very hungry, and it seems that we can not get enough of it. We eat and eat until we finally discover that we are somewhat uncomfortable. We feel sleepy and heavy, have a headache, or may even be ill after the meal. Indigestion may follow, with bitter doses of medicine.

Of course this manner of eating is not good for us. Whenever the stomach is given more food than it needs or can take care of without distress, harm has been done. We have in some degree injured our health.

Do you not think that stuffing ourselves in such a way also suggests somewhat the piggishness which we do not admire in our four-footed friends out in the

LEARNING TO EAT

pen? It is a good rule to continue eating until we are no longer really hungry, but to stop when we *could* still eat a little more.

Eating between meals.—What boy or girl has not sometimes become hungry between meals and run into the house begging mother for a "piece"! Under ordinary circumstances we should eat three good meals a day and not eat between meals.

One can see the reason for this when he knows that the stomach requires several hours of hard work to digest the meal we usually eat. New food taken into the stomach disturbs the digestion of the food already there.

Especially should we avoid the soda fountain habit. Of course we may like the good things that are sold there, but we would be much better off without most of them. They are bad for the digestion, and they spoil our appetite for the next meal. The soda fountain habit also leads us to spend money which would be better used for other things.

"Piecing" between meals is not a good habit

Learning to control our desires.—We sometimes like a certain article of food that does not agree with us. Surely most of us can think of some such foods.

One schoolgirl remarked in my hearing that chocolate creams always made her sick, but that she liked them so well she was going to eat some. Do you not think she was rather weak and foolish?

We may like peanuts or fudge or pickles, but that is no reason for eating them if they do not agree with us. We should be the masters of our appetites and not let them control us!

Coffee and tea are not good drinks for us during the period of our growth. They are not true foods. They contain stimulants which the young do not need, and they have almost no nourishment to add to our growth or strength. Milk should be the chief drink with our meals. Every boy and girl who drinks coffee and tea instead of milk is hindering growth and full development.

Learning to like certain foods.—There are certain foods that we must *learn* to like. When we first try them we do not like them, but after eating them for a time they become very palatable to us. I have a young friend who does not like potatoes. Another boy I know eats almost no vegetables; he says he does not like them. Perhaps some who study this book may not like eggs; others may balk at drinking milk; and still others may avoid meat.

Often our dislike for some common article of food is a mere whim, or comes because we have not eaten it long enough to *learn* to like it. It is more than likely

LEARNING TO EAT

that we could cure most of our dislikes of this kind by simply determining that we will eat the food, and that we will learn to like it.

We should try to like all the common foods that other people are daily eating. We should have as few dislikes as possible. Cultivating the habit of eating many different varieties of food will give us better range for our diet. It will also save us from being finicky, and from making unnecessary trouble for those who provide our meals.

Interesting things to do.—1. Make a list of the foods you do not like. Which of these are especially desirable foods? Are you willing to try learning to like them?

2. Make a list of any foods that seem to disagree with you. Are you willing to keep from eating such foods?

3. Are you in the habit of piecing between meals? If so, suppose you try eating just a little more at meal time and then determine not to eat between meals even if you do get hungry. You can soon break yourself of the bad habit.

Good habits to form.—The following are some of the eating habits especially to be cultivated:

Being quiet, orderly, dainty, cheerful and happy at the table.

Learning to eat the foods others eat unless we find some that disagree with us.

Refusing to eat things we know are not good for us, even if we like them. This may include coffee or tea, candy, ice-cream cones or other such things between meals.

Stopping short of over-eating even with foods we greatly like.

Health Problems

1. Report on Health Chores.
2. When Margaret came home from the party she told her mother that she had had a good time except that she sat beside Jimmie at supper and that he "ate like a little pig." What ought Jimmie to do about it?
3. Tom said he had a good time at the party except that he ate too much and was uncomfortable. What do you suppose the hostess thought about Tom's eating?
4. How long should you chew each mouthful of food?
5. Suppose you were asked to make five rules about how to conduct oneself at the table, what would they be?
6. Last year Harry said he did not like either beets or celery. This year he likes both. He has *learned* to like them. What foods have you *learned* to like?
7. What bad table habits have you observed (do not give names), and how should they be corrected?
8. Are you at present trying to form any new good habits about eating, or to break any bad ones?

CHAPTER IX

GOOD AND BAD MICROBES

Everybody has read fairy stories, and knows that some fairies are good and some are bad. It is likely that fairies are altogether make-believe, but I want to tell you a true story as wonderful as any fairy story. This is about tiny creatures that we call *microbes*.

The microbes are all about us, though so small that we can not see them without a microscope. They float in the air; we draw many of them into the lungs with every breath. They swarm in the water we drink. They are found in our food. Hundreds of them are sticking to the feet of the fly which alights on our dish.

Where microbes are found.—Microbes are also found in the soil. They cling to our bodies, and attach themselves to our clothing. They even enter our bodies, and are found in our blood, in our stomach, and in our lungs. They get into a scratch or a cut and cause it to fester. In fact it would be hard to find anywhere in the world a nook or corner which does not serve as the home for many millions of these very small beings.

Now some of the microbes belong to the animal kingdom, but most of them are plants. We shall be interested in our story chiefly in plant microbes, one great group of which are called *bacteria*. Whether we use the word *microbe* or the word *bacteria*, then you are to think of tiny plants too small to be seen.

The work of microbes.—Most bacteria are harmless, but a few bring us disease. Most help in producing our food, while a few kinds rob us of our food by taking it for themselves.

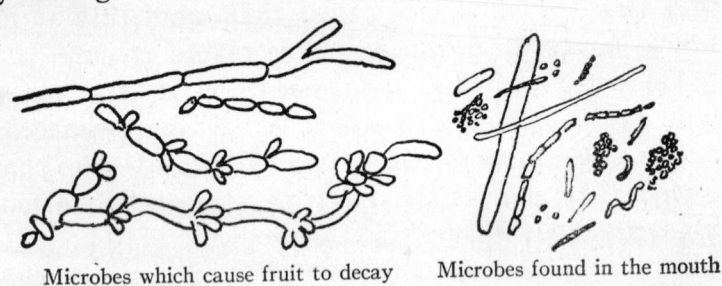

Microbes which cause fruit to decay   Microbes found in the mouth

Yesterday I saw an example of the work of some of these robber plants. A small friend of mine was rummaging about the pantry shelf, possibly looking for the cookies. She found a piece of bread that had fallen behind a box and lain for several days in a warm, moist place. The bread was all covered over with a soft, furry looking growth that her mother told her was *mold*.

The mold consists of a tiny forest of very small and nearly colorless plants. The spores (or seeds) of these

GOOD AND BAD MICROBES

little plants are everywhere floating in the air, and some of them had fallen on the piece of bread. They at once started to grow, like plants in your garden, and the bread was soon covered with a mass of mold. The mold plants were using the bread for their food, that was all.

Difference between bacteria and green plants. —There are many different kinds of bacteria, probably as many as there are of the green plants we see about us. But bacteria are all alike in one thing— they lack the substance called chlorophyl (klō′ rŏ fĭl) which makes the world of visible plants green.

The color itself does not seem to be so very important, but the chlorophyl which causes the green color makes all the difference in the world. For it is the chlorophyl that enables the green plant to take its food from the air, the sunshine, the soil and water.

The importance of this is readily understood when we stop to think that all the food for both animals and plants must come from these sources. No animal can get its food directly from air, sunshine, soil and water. Only plants can do this. *Nor can any plant get its food in this way which does not have chlorophyl.*

What bacteria live upon.—But bacteria that our story deals with all lack chlorophyl. Only a few can live on air, sunshine and soil. The others must, just like ourselves, have *organic* food; that is, food coming from plants or the flesh of animals.

This means that the bacteria must use the same foods that we use. Meat, vegetables, eggs, milk, fruit—these are foods we must have. But they are also the foods most favored by the bacteria. And there is therefore a constant battle to see which will get the food, we or our bacteria enemies.

For example, you pick a dozen choice apples and lay them away to ripen for Thanksgiving. When you come to get them you find that half of them have

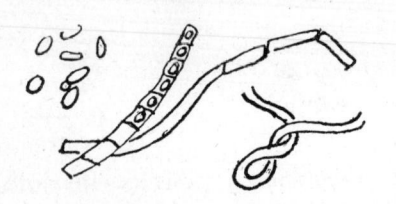

Microbes found in the soil

Microbes which cause meat to decay

decayed and are not fit to be eaten. What has happened? The bacteria got ahead of you! One of the apples may have had a tiny break in the skin when you laid them away. The bacteria immediately attacked this point and began their growth. It was their work that caused the decay of your apples.

Bacteria attacking our foods.—If we set away a roast of meat where the air is warm and moist enough for bacteria to grow, the meat soon "spoils." This only means that the bacteria have set at work upon the meat and used it for their food.

GOOD AND BAD MICROBES

Bacteria sometimes get into the fruit we can and cause it to "work" so that it spoils. They swarm into our sweet cider and make it "hard." They attack our bottle of sweet milk and it has soon soured. In fact there is almost no article of our food that they do not seek to appropriate.

Not satisfied with trying to get our food from us, the microbes even attack our bodies. Some of them live upon our skin, and cause such diseases as *ring-worm*. Others inhabit the stomach and intestines. Still others

Microbes which cause diphtheria

Microbes which cause grippe

Microbes which cause bubonic plague

live in the mouth, feeding upon the particles of food left on the teeth and causing them to decay.

Bacteria and disease.—Our worst microbe enemies are certain kinds that cause diseases when once they secure a hold within the body. We often speak of these microbes as "disease germs." Let a certain kind of germ set up its growth in our lungs, and we soon have tuberculosis. Another kind brings us diphtheria, another scarlet fever, another measles, another is responsible for colds, sore throats, and pneumonia. And so on throughout most other diseases that cause us so much trouble.

We are in a constant battle with the disease germs that threaten us. But if we follow a few simple directions for keeping well and strong we have little cause for fear, for with right habits of living we can win in the battle most of the time.

Bacteria that are our friends.—Nor must we make the mistake of thinking that all bacteria are our enemies. They are like the fairies, the most are good and a few are bad. Or they are like the green plants that grow round about us, some are friends and some are enemies.

Some of the most friendly microbes live in the soil. Without them we could not raise our crops. Others work in the cream and make it ready for churning, and still others give the delicate flavor to butter.

We could not make cheese without microbes. The vinegar we use is a microbe product. Microbes immediately set at work upon any bit of refuse or dead matter. They cause it to decay, and soon make it harmless. With this decayed matter they feed the plants. In these and a score of other ways certain kinds of bacteria are good fairies.

Perhaps we may say of microbes, like the "little girl with a curl"—when they are good they are very good, and when they are bad they are horrid!

Interesting things to do.—1. You can easily try an interesting experiment in growing a crop of mold. Put a piece of bread or of apple on a

GOOD AND BAD MICROBES

plate and cover it over with a glass. The air must be somewhat moist. Now set away for several days in a rather dark place, since molds do not grow so well in the light. Study the mold, when it has appeared, with a magnifying-glass.

2. Squeeze the juice out of an apple and set it away in a warm place for several days. Has it become sour? What causes it to sour? If you will put a few drops of acid in the apple juice it will not sour, because the acid kills the bacteria. This is the way sweet cider is kept from becoming "hard."

3. The bacteria that cause diphtheria and other diseases are sometimes found in the mouths of healthy persons. Decaying teeth are swarming with bacteria. Do you think, then, that it is a good habit to put pencils or pens into our mouths to act as carriers of these germs? Watch yourself to see whether you have this habit.

Health Problems

1. After reading this lesson what reasons can you give why a common drinking cup should not be used at school or other public places?
2. A closed tank for drinking water at a school was not cleaned out for several weeks. Then it was found to have a bad smell. How do you suppose the bad smell was caused?

CHAPTER X

PROTECTING OUR FOOD FROM MICROBES

Last week a friend invited me to visit with him a great packing plant from which tons of beef, pork and mutton are daily shipped to the city markets.

After watching the various processes by which the meat is prepared, we were taken into a room where we were given heavy overcoats to put on. Then we were led into the large refrigerating rooms where the meat is kept in cold storage.

Here we saw great quantities of meat hanging on large racks many feet in length. Although the weather was warm outside, the room was so cold that we could see our breath, and frost hung thick on the walls.

Our guide told us that the carcasses of beef, pork and mutton were often kept for months in these cold storage rooms before being shipped to the markets for our tables.

Why we keep food in the refrigerator.—One might think that meat kept so long would spoil, but it does not. In fact it would remain sweet and fresh for years if the temperature of the storage room was kept slightly below the freezing point. For in this low

PROTECTING OUR FOOD FROM MICROBES 73

temperature bacteria can not grow, and without bacteria the meat will not spoil.

We use the same principle in our home refrigerators as in the cold storage rooms of the packing plant. True, we can not cool our refrigerators to the freezing point with ice. But we can make them so cool that the growth of the bacteria is very slow. Foods will therefore keep in them for several days without spoiling.

Why dried foods will not spoil.—Not only must bacteria have warmth for their growth, but they must also have moisture. In certain desert or arid regions where the air is very dry, meat and other foods can be kept in the open air without spoiling.

On the dry plains of Arizona fresh meat is hung up in the sunshine, where it quickly "cures" by drying.

The black specks show the germs revealed by the microscope on a drinking glass which had been used by many people in a public place. A small section of the glass, when put under a more powerful magnifier, showed the swarm of germs appearing in the next picture

The atmosphere has so little moisture that bacteria do not grow readily enough to cause the meat to decay.

One of the most common methods of defeating bacteria is by drying our foods so that the bacteria can not grow upon them. Great quantities of fruits and vegetables are preserved in this way every year.

Once such foods are well dried, they may be safely packed away without fear of the bacteria.

Defeating bacteria by canning foods.—When we can our fruit or vegetables, we first boil them. This not only cooks the food, but also kills all the bacteria. While the product we are canning is still very hot, we seal the jar or can quickly so that fresh bacteria can not enter. If we do our work successfully, the fruit or vegetables will then keep as long as we wish.

If canned fruit or vegetables spoil in the cans, we may know that some bacteria were left alive when the food was canned, or else that they have got in after the canning was completed, and have set up their growth.

You may have noticed that when a can of fruit begins to ferment soon after it is canned, your mother sometimes empties it out and cooks it over again. She then cans it a second time. The cooking process kills the bacteria which had begun their work. If no fresh ones are allowed to enter, the fruit will keep.

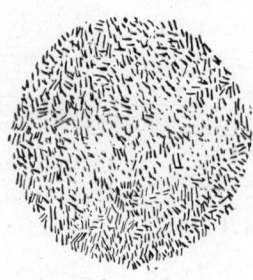

A highly magnified section from the drinking glass shown on page 73. These are germs left from the lips of many persons who drank from the glass. Who wants to take into his mouth the germs coming from the mouths of others?

Cleanliness an enemy of bacteria.—Fresh milk that is put into bottles or cans which have had sour

PROTECTING OUR FOOD FROM MICROBES

milk in them will sour very quickly if the bottles or cans are not thoroughly washed and scalded. This is because the particles of the sour milk contain millions of bacteria, which immediately begin to work in the new milk. This starts it to souring.

Any dish into which food is put must therefore be perfectly clean if we wish the food to keep. Not only must the ordinary dust and dirt be removed, but also the bacteria which might start the food to decay.

Two ways to kill bacteria.—A number of different kinds of disease germs are often carried in water or in milk. A recent epidemic of typhoid fever was traced to the milk coming from a certain dairy. Typhoid germs had got into the water with which the milk cans and pails were washed, and were thus carried to the customers who bought the milk. This caused the death of a number of people.

Another typhoid epidemic was traced to the germs from a sewer which overflowed into the water supply of a city.

Tuberculosis is often carried to children in the milk which comes from tubercular cows.

If there is any suspicion that germs have got into the water supply, the water should be boiled before it is drunk. Milk that contains disease germs should be boiled or *pasteurized*.

To pasteurize milk it is kept at a temperature of 149 degrees Fahrenheit for twenty minutes, or 176 degrees for five minutes. This heating is sufficient to kill the germs of tuberculosis.

Interesting problems to solve.—1. Having in mind that the tiny plants that we call bacteria require warmth and moisture for their growth the same as green plants, see whether you can answer these questions:

(a) Why do we store our winter supply of apples and potatoes in a cool, dry place?

(b) Why do peaches, pears, apples and other fruit sometimes rot on the trees in a very wet, hot season?

(c) Why will dried beef or potato chips keep without spoiling?

2. A young man I knew was out hunting with a companion. They became very thirsty, and my friend proposed that they drink from a small creek they were crossing. His companion objected that it was not very clean, but my friend drank. In about two weeks he came down with typhoid, from which he died. It was later found that drainage reached this stream from a place where there was typhoid. What would this case suggest to you about drinking from streams or ponds?

3. Why will milk put into a can that has not been thoroughly cleaned, sour more quickly than if put in a can that has been scalded?

CHAPTER XI

WHY WE SHOULD GET RID OF FLIES

A friend remarked to me the other day that "swat the fly" has become the great American motto. Certain it is at least that we have declared war on the fly.

Let us give the fly no quarter. For flies are always our enemies. They are themselves dirty, and they are carriers of filth. They breed in vile refuse. They eat everything that is repulsive and unclean, and they always have filthy feet.

The fly is always dirty.—The fly that comes sipping out of the edge of your glass of milk, or the one that comes crawling over the sugar on your berry dish has probably come from the dirtiest things imaginable directly to your dinner table. No wonder that we want to "swat the fly."

Flies are not only dirty, but they also carry disease germs. The flies that you see swarming over the fruit which the peddler or grocer has for sale may just have come from drinking out of the sewer. And the sewer may contain the germs of typhoid fever.

HYGIENE AND HEALTH

The fly carries disease.—Such germs cling to the fly's feet and mouth; he can carry hundreds of them. These he distributes over the fruit when he crawls upon it. Then if you buy the fruit and eat it without cleaning it, you are in danger of taking these typhoid

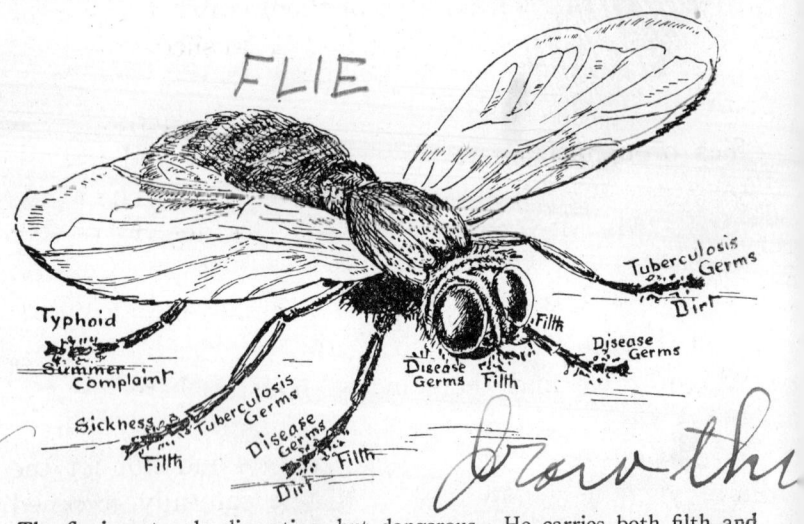

The fly is not only disgusting, but dangerous. He carries both filth and disease about with him

or other germs into your mouth and contracting the disease.

There is no doubt that hundreds and perhaps thousands of people are killed every year by diseases which are carried by the flies.

The other day I was walking along the street and came upon a disgusting mass of sputum which some-

WHY WE SHOULD GET RID OF FLIES 79

body had spit from his mouth after coughing. There were a dozen flies around the edge of it eating the horrid stuff. When they were disturbed by some one coming past, they flew away and half of them immediately alighted upon fruit in a peddler's cart at the edge of the sidewalk. Two of them crawled inside the open mouth of a sack of candy and finished their meal upon it.

Who knows how many tuberculosis germs those flies brought from their disgusting meal and tracked over the apples and candy which children would afterwards eat! Not only should we get rid of flies as fast as we can, but we should never eat food that has been exposed where flies can get at it.

Shutting the flies out.—Besides "swatting" flies wherever we find them in our houses, there are two other ways of getting rid of them. One way is to have screens upon our doors and windows and not let the flies get in. Our houses should be carefully screened whenever the flies are bad.

But a still better way than either "swatting" them or shutting them out is to quit raising them. With a little care on the part of everybody it would be very easy to get rid of all the flies, so that there would be hardly one left to trouble us.

Preventing flies from hatching.—For flies always hatch in filth or some decaying matter. The mother fly lays her eggs preferably in a pile of manure. If

HYGIENE AND HEALTH

manure is not at hand, a rotting straw stack or some other filth will do.

Flies hatch in manure or rubbish, live upon all that is filthy, and then come to our tables and get into our food

In about ten days the eggs hatch into worm-like maggots. After a little time the maggots grow wings and legs and become full-grown flies.

WHY WE SHOULD GET RID OF FLIES

Now since flies are so short-lived, few of them living over the first winter, it is clear that if we can stop hatching fly eggs, we shall soon be without flies. And since it takes the eggs from a week to ten days to hatch out in a manure pile, it is evident that if the manure from our stables, or other rubbish in which flies hatch, is cleared away promptly, then the flies' eggs would not have a chance to hatch.

In cities where laws have been passed requiring that all rubbish shall be kept cleaned up and hauled away or burned, it has been found that after a year or two there are few flies left. What flies still remain are hatched in rubbish heaps which have in some way escaped notice of the health officers.

How boys and girls can help.—But as long as there are flies it is the duty of every boy and girl to help shut them out of our homes, and to help trap and kill them when they get inside. And of course we shall always want to see that no food is left uncovered where flies can get it. For nobody wants to eat after a fly!

Fruit, vegetables, bread or other food should not be left uncovered in stores and markets so that flies can get at it. Many states and cities now have laws requiring that foods offered for sale in the markets shall be kept in cases away from the flies. What is the law in your state or town? Are foods in the markets protected from flies?

HYGIENE AND HEALTH

Facts to remember about flies.—1. Flies always leave filth of one kind or another on our food when they crawl over it. For flies hatch in filth, live in filth, eat filth.

2. Flies are one of the most dangerous carriers of disease germs. We should never eat food that has come from markets where there are flies, unless we first clean the food.

3. Most flies are hatched in manure piles. Clean up the manure every two weeks or oftener, and there will be few flies. It is possible that this can not always be done around barns in the country, but it can in towns and cities.

Health Problems

1. Why are flies so much more plentiful late in the season than early in the season?
2. A certain town which has many dirty alleys and barns with manure heaps is offering a prize for trapping flies. Another town near by has a law against dirty alleys and manure heaps. Which town is more likely to rid itself of flies?
3. Notice the market places and shops of your town to see how many places protect the food for sale from flies. Ought this question to make any difference where you do your buying?
4. If you live in the country, what can you do to prevent the hatching of flies? Talk with your father and mother about this.

CHAPTER XII

PROTECTION AGAINST MOSQUITOES

Mosquitoes have always been looked upon as enemies because their sting is so unpleasant. The poison in their sting also causes lumps to swell on the skin of many people.

A very much worse crime than this has been fastened upon mosquitoes, however. The mosquito has been found to be the carrier of yellow fever, malaria, and perhaps other diseases. The way this crime was proved on the mosquito is an interesting story.

Yellow fever carried by mosquitoes.—When in the year 1898 the United States was at war with Spain, our army was stationed in Cuba where yellow fever was raging. The army doctors already believed the mosquito to be the carrier of yellow fever. They determined to find out for sure whether it was carried by mosquitoes from yellow fever patients to well persons, or whether the disease was caught by germs carried in the air or upon clothing.

So the army doctors built a small house, and screened all its windows and doors to keep mosquitoes out. They brought straight from the beds of patients

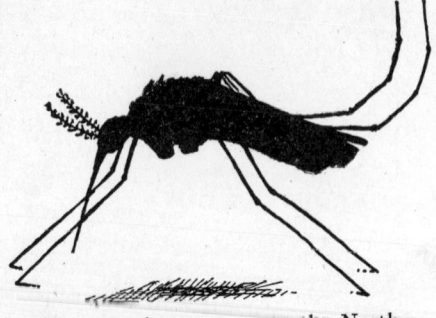

84 HYGIENE AND HEALTH

smitten with yellow fever soiled sheets, pillow cases and blankets to use as bedding. A number of brave soldiers volunteered to live in this house and use the bedding from the yellow fever patients. They stayed here for about three weeks, but not one of them took the disease.

The mosquito common to the North. Note the position of the body and legs when at rest

The doctors then obtained another house in which everything was as clean as could be, with not an article in it that had been near yellow fever. In this house were placed another brave group of soldiers, ready to risk their lives to find out the truth about yellow fever and the mosquitoes.

Mosquitoes were allowed to suck the blood of yellow fever patients and then were turned loose in the room where the soldiers were.

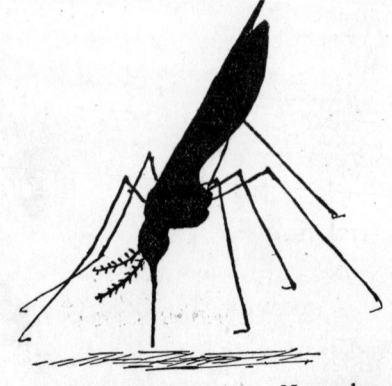

The malaria mosquito. Note the position of the body and legs

PROTECTION AGAINST MOSQUITOES 85

More than half of those bitten by the yellow fever mosquitoes took the disease, and some of them died. Do you not think that these soldiers were true heroes!

Another count against mosquitoes.—Another disease known as *malaria*, or fever and ague, is carried by mosquitoes. For many years it has been known that malaria occurs more or less in all warm climates, especially in hot weather after rains and near marshes where water stands stagnant. It was formerly thought that the disease was taken by breathing air poisoned in some way by the hot, stagnant marshes. But finally it was discovered that only the mosquitoes are to blame for carrying malaria.

When the building of the Panama Canal was undertaken by the United States, it was at first difficult to get workmen. They were afraid of malaria and yellow fever. And they had good right to be, for thousands of people died in this region every year from these diseases.

Getting rid of mosquitoes.—But Surgeon General Gorgas undertook to drive the mosquitoes out so that it might be safe for our workmen. He drained the marshes. He poured oil upon ponds and in ditches which could not be drained. In every way possible he destroyed the breeding places of mosquitoes. He soon got ahead of the mosquitoes, and Panama region was made as healthful as any part of our own country. Yellow fever and malaria almost disappeared.

There is a certain kind of a mosquito that carries yellow fever, and another kind that carries malaria. The former of these mosquitoes can not live except in very warm climates, but we find the malaria mosquito in the northern states as well as in the South. Mosquitoes of any kind are undesirable, however, and should not be allowed where it is possible to destroy them.

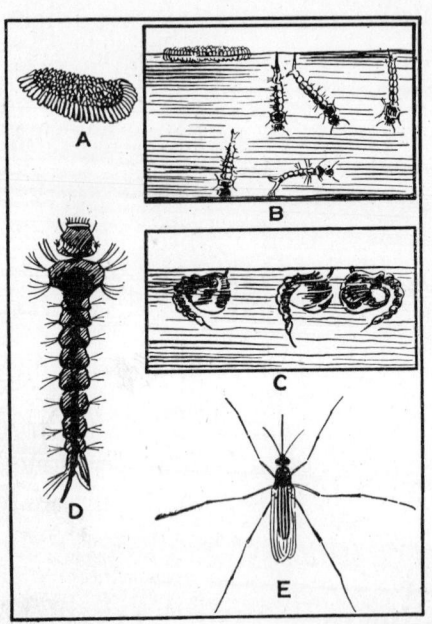

A. A mass of mosquito eggs. B. Mosquito larvæ (wrigglers) which have hatched from the eggs. C and D. Stages of growth. E. The mosquito

Breeding places of mosquitoes.—Mosquitoes breed in stagnant water, in ponds, ditches, puddles, rain barrels, or even open vessels or dishes of water outside.

The wrigglers that you have seen in the rain barrel after it has stood for ten days or two weeks, are the larvæ of mosquitoes. They will soon hatch out and be flying about stinging you as a reward for having allowed them to hatch.

PROTECTION AGAINST MOSQUITOES

Helping destroy mosquitoes.—Boys and girls can help prevent mosquitoes around their homes by seeing that there is no stagnant water left unscreened for them to get into. Puddles can be filled with dirt. Small ditches can be opened to allow the water to drain off. Small ponds where mosquitoes breed may have a little kerosene poured on them. This will kill the larvæ and no mosquitoes will hatch.

Facts to remember about mosquitoes.—1. Yellow fever and malaria are carried by mosquitoes. Where there are no mosquitoes there is no yellow fever nor malaria.

2. Mosquitoes are an annoyance even when they do not carry disease. Their stings contain enough poison to cause swelling and soreness on the flesh of most persons.

3. Mosquitoes hatch in swamps, marshes, pools and puddles, or other stagnant water. Even a rain barrel or a can of water may serve as a hatching place for hundreds of them. To get rid of mosquitoes, prevent their hatching.

Health Problems

1. It has been noticed that as a new region of country is settled and the land drained and put under cultivation, there are fewer mosquitoes. Why?
2. There are more mosquitoes during rainy seasons than dry seasons. Why?
3. Are you keeping up with the Health Chores?
4. Have you noticed mosquitoes at your home? If so, try to find out where they come from.

CHAPTER XIII

THE AIR AND BREATHING

Why does a person drown when he is under water? Surely the water itself does not hurt the lungs. No, what the water does is to shut the air out of the lungs. It is the want of air that really causes the death of the drowning person.

We eat only three times a day. We drink water every two or three hours. But we must breathe air into our lungs every moment day and night as long as we live.

Experiments in breathing.—Sit down with a watch before you. Breathe naturally, and count the number of times you breathe in one minute. About eighteen or twenty times? If you try holding your breath, you find after a few seconds that you become very uncomfortable. You are obliged to give it up and go to breathing again. No one can live for more than a few minutes without air.

Since air is so necessary for our lives, it is well that it is so plentiful. We live at the bottom of a great ocean of air, as fish live in the ocean of water.

This air ocean is so deep that it extends upward

THE AIR AND BREATHING

scores of miles above the earth. We find it everywhere. It sweeps about us in great currents that we call winds and storms. It creeps through the doors and windows into our houses. It passes through our clothing and bathes the body. It fills every corner, nook, and crevice all about us. It even finds its way into the soil and helps in the growth of plants.

Air enough for all.—One would think that because air is so plentiful and so free, every one might have all the air he needs. Yet there are many people who do not get enough good air, and who are suffering for want of it as they would starve for want of food.

Those who work in poorly ventilated shops or down in mines show by their pale faces that they do not get good air. The crowded street-car with its windows all closed, the stuffy school room, or the bedroom in which the windows are not opened at night is robbing us of the air we need for our health and growth.

What the air does for the body.—The air that we take into the lungs does two important things for us: it supplies the body with *oxygen*, and it carries away *carbon dioxide*.

The fire that burns in your furnace is produced by the oxygen of the air uniting with the carbon of the coal. When you want your fire to burn faster you let in more oxygen by opening the draft; when you want it to burn more slowly you shut out the oxygen. If you shut out all the oxygen the fire will go out.

Oxygen is as necessary to our bodies as it is to the fire in the furnace. No living thing can exist without it. The more oxygen an animal breathes the more actively alive it is. If you will catch a mouse and put it into a jar to which has been added an extra amount of oxygen, you will be surprised at the liveliness of your mouse. It will jump and dance and spring about and be very merry indeed. The extra oxygen makes it very much alive.

How the oxygen works.—The oxygen that is breathed into the lungs is picked up by little red bodies in the blood, called *corpuscles*, and carried to every part of the body. Wherever worn-out or dead tissue is found, the oxygen unites with the carbon of the dead tissue precisely as it does with the coal in the furnace, and burns it up. It is this burning up of the body's worn-out tissues that makes the tiny fires mentioned in a preceding chapter. And it is these fires that keep up the heat of the body.

The fire burning in the furnace produces a gas, which escapes up the chimney. This gas is *carbon dioxide*. The burning up of the waste tissues in the body by the action of oxygen produces carbon dioxide exactly like that from the furnace.

Getting rid of carbon dioxide.—This carbon dioxide is carried by the blood to the lungs, where it is

THE AIR AND BREATHING

breathed out with the air that is expelled. If it is not properly removed from the body it acts as a poison just as if one should breathe coal gas or illuminating gas. If you treat the mouse in your jar to air containing too much carbon dioxide it will soon curl up in the bottom of the jar and die.

The amount of oxygen supplied the body and the amount of carbon dioxide removed depends on two things:

(1) Whether we have an abundance of pure fresh air to breathe.

(2) The size of our lungs and how we use them in breathing.

The size of our lungs.—If your lungs are well developed they should be able to hold about five pints of air when they are entirely full. If you have stooped shoulders and a hollow chest, if you do not breathe deeply, or if you do not exercise freely in the open air it is possible that your lungs do not hold more than four pints, or even three pints.

One whose lungs are not doing their work well can never be up to his full strength and vigor. He lacks endurance. He takes cold easily, and is subject to diseases in general. He is more liable to tuberculosis, for it is in the little used portions of the lungs that the disease germs begin their work.

It is worth while to know how to breathe right. Press your hands against your body just below the ribs. When you breathe clear to the bottom of your lungs you can feel the body expand at this point. If you fill only the upper part of your lungs, you will feel little or no expansion. Be sure to force the air to the very bottom of your lungs.

Giving our lungs a fair chance.—It is well to take several minutes now and then for deep breathing. While standing in the fresh air, see how full you can fill your lungs, and how deep you can make the air go down. But better still is to form the habit of breathing deep and full all the time. This will require that we be careful not to sit or stand in such postures that the lungs will be crowded or cramped.

Best of all, however, is plenty of good exercise in the open air. Run a block at your best clip, or take a running start and see how far you can jump. Then notice how deep and full you are breathing.

Count the rate of your breathing just before and just after such exercise. Do you not think that all the cells of your lungs are sure to be put into use when you run or play or work? Exercise also makes our tissues hungry for oxygen, so that what the lungs take in is freely used.

Adenoids.—Sometimes a growth called an *adenoid* occurs at the back part of the nose cavity. This hinders breathing and causes one to breathe through his mouth. Besides interfering with proper breathing, adenoids are bad for the health in other ways, and

THE AIR AND BREATHING

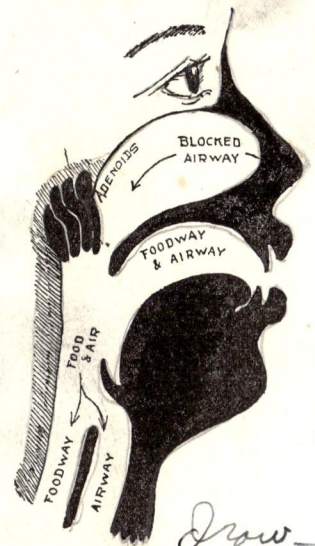

Note the growth of adenoids at the back of the nose cavity, and how they block the passage way of air to the lungs

should be removed by the doctor. This can be done without much trouble or pain.

If one finds difficulty in breathing with his mouth closed either day or night, he should have his nose examined for an adenoid. Adenoids hinder the growth, make one dull mentally, injure the shape of the mouth, and make the face and eyes take on a stupid expression.

Questions and experiments.—1. Do you often have a cold in your head? Does your nose get stopped up, so that it is hard to breathe? Do your nose passages ever feel dry and burning? If any of these troubles occur often you should have the doctor examine your nose. Some simple treatment taken in time might save you serious trouble later.

2. One of the best tests of health and vigor is the amount of air one's lungs will hold. This is measured by an instrument called the *spirometer* (spī-rŏm'-e-ter). One blows into the spirometer tube and the record shows how many cubic

inches of air he can force out in one breath. If there is a spirometer available, test your lung capacity.

3. Another test of the capacity of your lungs is the number of inches you can expand your chest. Have some one hold a tape line drawn rather snugly around your chest just under the arms. Take your measure first with all the air breathed out, making your chest just as small as possible. Then take your measure again while you breathe your lungs very full, making your chest as large as you can. The difference between these two measures is your chest expansion. Compare your expansion with the table below:

Chest expansion for boys should be:

At 10 years of age.................. 2.75 inches
At 11 years of age.................. 2.90 inches
At 12 years of age.................. 3.05 inches
At 13 years of age.................. 3.25 inches

Chest expansion for girls should be:

At 10 years of age.................. 2.4 inches
At 11 years of age.................. 2.6 inches
At 12 years of age.................. 2.45 inches
At 13 years of age.................. 2.6 inches

CHAPTER XIV

LIVING IN GOOD AIR

Air that has been breathed and re-breathed several times is no longer capable of sustaining life. Following the battle of Austerlitz three hundred Austrian prisoners were shut up in a little prison far too small for the number, and with but little ventilation. Within one day two hundred and sixty of them had died from heat and the want of fresh air.

Another instance of this kind occurred in 1848 when the master of an English ship shut one hundred steerage passengers in a room not more than half the size of an ordinary school room. They soon became frantic for want of air, and seventy-two of them had died before they forced their way out of the room.

The "Black Hole" of Calcutta is the name given to a prison in Calcutta where years ago the Hindoos shut one hundred and forty-six British prisoners whom they had captured in battle. The room where they were imprisoned was small and had only two windows. They soon felt the lack of air, and the stronger fought their way to the windows. When morning came only twenty-three were left alive.

Suffering for want of air.—Of course, we no longer treat prisoners in this way. It is very seldom indeed that a person dies directly from lack of enough air to breathe. We may all suffer greatly in health and strength, however, from over-crowded school rooms, moving picture houses that are packed too full, or even from several persons sleeping in a bedroom that does not have its windows open.

Plenty of open air is so important to our health and to the development of our minds that nearly every large city now has what are called "open-air school rooms." These rooms are built with one side entirely open or else with windows so fixed that the entire side of the room can be thrown open.

Open-air schools.—In these open-air rooms are placed the children who have some sickness or who are backward in their studies, so that it is especially necessary for them to have plenty of good air to breathe. The boys and girls are bundled up warmly and here they get their lessons just as if they were in an ordinary school room.

It has been found that boys and girls always do better work in the open-air schools than they do in the closed school rooms. They also improve in health and gain rapidly in weight and strength. If plenty of fresh air is good for those who are sick or backward, do you not think it is just as necessary for those who are well and strong?

LIVING IN GOOD AIR

Giving the skin fresh air.—The skin requires an abundance of fresh air, just as do the lungs. The story is told that years ago at some great festival a child was wanted to represent an angel. They took a small boy and coated his body over closely on the

An open-air school in winter-time. The warm wraps and hoods keep the children as comfortable as in a heated school room, though the snow lies deep outside

skin with gold foil. After a few hours it was found that the child had died. He had had plenty of air for his lungs, but he also needed air for his skin, and also his skin could not do its other work with every pore clogged up.

Between the clothing and the body there is constantly a thin blanket of air. This air soon becomes heated to the temperature of the body and also grows impure from the waste matter that comes through the skin.

Good ventilation requires moving air.—You may have noticed that if you become tired and sleepy from sitting in a close room, you feel wonderfully refreshed

School in the open air, where both lungs and skin can have all they need—no dust, no dirt, no germs

when the window is thrown open and a current of air is allowed to pour through the room. This feeling of refreshment is caused not more by the air that comes to the lungs than by that which flows over the surface of the body.

Good ventilation therefore requires a moving current of air in the room. This current need not be

LIVING IN GOOD AIR

strong enough that we shall feel a draft, but it must be sufficient to change the layer of air next the body.

One of the best ways to secure a moving current of air in a room is by having an open fireplace, through which a current of air constantly passes up the chimney and out of the room. A window may be opened slightly at the bottom on one side of the room, and another window opened at the top on another side, thus creating a current across the room.

Air that is too dry.—It is possible to have the air in our houses too dry to be good for the lungs or the skin. When our houses are heated by stoves and furnaces, or by steam radiators in the winter-time, the air usually becomes so dry that furniture, doors, and other wood-work shrink and show cracks.

Whenever the air dries out in this way it is bad for the throat and lungs. It makes the membranes of the nose feel dry and smarting. We are then more liable to colds, catarrh, pneumonia, tonsillitis, and other troubles.

How to keep air moist.—If we have steam radiators, we can hang at the back of the radiator an open pan of water to evaporate in the room. The water pan should be fitted into our hot-air furnaces so that the vapor may come into the room with the air. Pans of water may also be set in the registers so that it will evaporate into the room. If a stove or fireplace is running, it is well to keep a kettle of water over the fire so that the steam may escape and add to the moisture.

The *hygrometer* is an instrument for measuring the amount of moisture in the air. The air in our living

If all workmen had as clean and pleasant a place to work there would be less sickness

rooms should show about 60 degrees of moisture on the hygrometer.

The right temperature.—Many people keep the temperature of their rooms too high. When we are sitting still reading or studying, the air temperature should usually range from 65 to 68 degrees Fahrenheit. It should never pass 70. If we are moving about or working in a room the temperature may be still lower.

LIVING IN GOOD AIR

It is not necessary that the temperature shall remain the same at all times. We can become accustomed to a difference of as much as 10 degrees so that we will not feel any discomfort from it. If we thus become used to changing temperatures, we will not so easily take cold nor feel the discomforts when we go out-of-doors or are in places where the temperature is cooler than we are accustomed to.

Interesting questions and experiments.—1. The experts tell us that school rooms should have about two hundred and fifty cubic feet of air space for each pupil. It will be interesting for you to find out whether your school room meets this requirement. Measure the room, find the number of cubic feet it contains, and divide this number by the number of pupils. The quotient should be at least 250.

2. Do you ever notice any closeness, stuffiness, or bad odor when you come into the school room or into your living rooms at home? If so, this indicates poor ventilation. If the ventilation is not good, can you help plan how to improve it?

3. Let each member of the class make a record of the winter temperature of the living room of his home in the morning just before he comes to school each day for a week, do the same at noon, and also in the evening at a certain hour. At the end of one week of observations, compare the

results from the different homes to see whether the temperature is higher than it ought to be.

4. If you have this lesson when the furnaces are running, note whether the doors, casings and furniture in your home show the effect of drying out. If they do you may know that the air is too dry for good health.

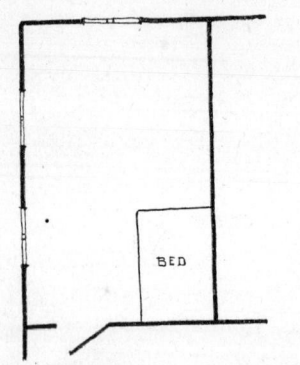

The *wrong* way to place a bed in the sleeping room. There is little circulation of air in the corner

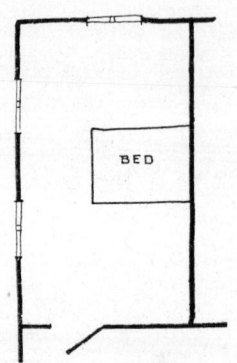

The *right* way to place a bed. The air will circulate freely over it

5. Moist air feels as warm at 60 degrees as very dry air feels at 70 degrees. What effect upon the amount of coal required to heat your home would it have to keep the air moist rather than to let it become too dry?

Good air habits.—Some good habits to form in connection with the study of this lesson are the following:

LIVING IN GOOD AIR

To live in an abundance of fresh air every moment, day and night whenever possible.

To see that there is a moving current of air in which you sit or work or sleep. Unless there is a special ventilating system this will require open windows or an open fireplace.

To train yourself to be comfortable if you are well and strong in a room in which the temperature is from 60 to 65 degrees.

To plan some way of adding moisture to the air in your home or school during the time when steam heat or furnaces are used.

Health Problems

1. Most cities forbid the use of any fuel that causes a heavy smoke. What reasons can you give in favor of such a law?
2. Are you getting enough good air to breathe: (1) at night, (2) at school? How do you know?
3. John boasts that he has not had a cold for over a year. George has a cold much of the time. John sleeps with his windows both wide open. George does not open his window in cold weather. Do you suppose the windows have something to do with it?
4. If you had to breathe a good deal of dust with the air you take into your lungs, would you rather breathe city or country dust? Why?

CHAPTER XV

THE HEART AND ITS WORK

You open the water faucet and the water comes rushing out of the pipes. But where does the power come from that makes the water pour out with such force? If you will trace the matter back to the water station, you will find there a pump, probably run by steam power. It is the pump that is driving the water through the pipes of the water system.

The heart, with the arteries and veins, is much like the water pump and the pipes that carry the water to our homes.

The heart a pump.—The heart is really a pump. It differs from the water pump, for it has within itself the power that does the pumping. The heart is a muscle about as big as your fist. It is located on the left side of the chest.

The heart never stops to rest; it rests between beats. It continues its work day and night without ceasing from the time we are born until we die. Every hour of the day, every minute, it is driving the blood through the arteries and veins all over the body.

The boys and girls who read this chapter have about

THE HEART AND ITS WORK

four quarts of blood in their bodies. Grown men have about six quarts.

The flow of the blood.—Put your finger on the pulse in your wrist and count the number of times the heart throbs in a minute. The throb of your pulse is the wave of blood in the artery caused by the beating of the heart, one throb for every heart beat. You will probably find that your heart is beating about eighty times in a minute.

At each beat the heart contracts and forces blood from its cavity out into the arteries. So rapidly and strongly does the heart work that all of the blood of your body makes the complete circuit about three times every minute. It takes a little longer for the blood to get clear around the body in a grown man, in whose body the

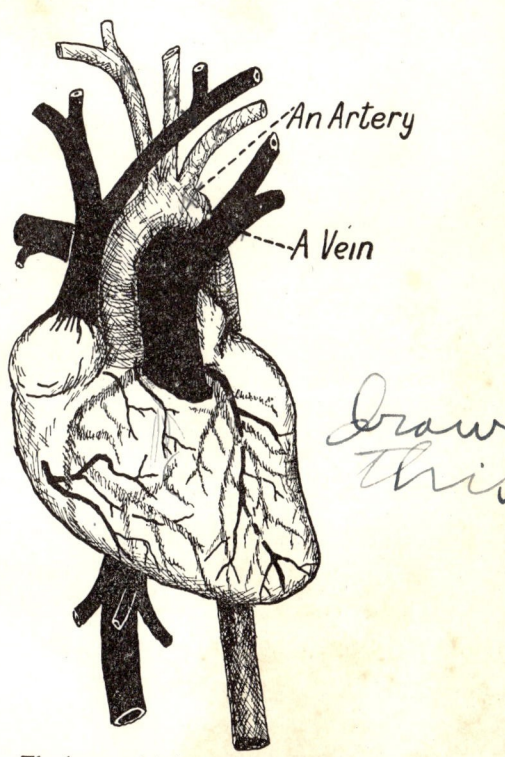

The heart with its arteries and veins

circuit is made only about two and one-half times in a minute.

When the body calls for more oxygen.—Everybody has noticed, of course, that the heart beats faster when we run or exercise than when we are sitting still. The heart increases in speed at such times because when we are exercising we are using up energy faster than when we are quiet. The tissues need more oxygen and there is more carbon dioxide to be removed. This means that the heart must work faster, so it speeds up.

Sometime when you have been running a race or playing hard in a game, you have got completely out of breath. Your lungs felt full, as if they were bursting. You simply could not get enough air to breathe. Perhaps your lungs had shooting pains in them.

Why we get out of breath.—Now this trouble does not originally come from the lungs, but from the heart. When the heart is able to give the lungs plenty of blood, one does not thus get out of breath. It would be fair to say, therefore, that our breath is as long as our heart is strong.

When we get badly out of breath, the heart is being over-worked and we need to be careful. If the heart is greatly over-strained, especially when we are young, it stretches the muscles. The beating of the heart is not so strong after this, and may cause us serious trouble.

THE HEART AND ITS WORK

Training the heart to its work.—There is little danger of over-working the heart, providing that we do not exercise too violently when we are not used to it. We should begin gradually in playing the harder games or running the races, and not exhaust ourselves too completely at first. The heart will soon become accustomed to its work and we shall have plenty of breath.

Without a heart that is able to force the blood strongly through his arteries and veins, one can not be sturdy and well. A weak heart and poor circulation leaves us pale, with little strength and endurance.

I knew a college student who had been ill and was unable to run more than a few rods without his heart beating violently and his breath becoming very short. He went to the doctor about it, and the doctor told him that what he must do was to train his heart gradually. So the doctor had him start by walking a block rather briskly, and end by running two rods. The next day the doctor told him, he could run a little farther, and the day after a little farther still, and so on, until finally his heart would be strong enough to stand severe exercise.

How to train the heart.—My friend faithfully followed the doctor's directions, and within a year was able to compete with other runners on the track. He kept on developing his heart and lung power until finally he won in an important long distance race.

School boys and girls need to train their hearts. Because they sit still most of the day, they should get out in the open air all they can when not in school. They should race or play or work until the heart throbs and the blood courses through the body. They should develop heart and lung power until they can run a block or play a game without getting out of breath.

Interesting things to do.—1. Show how to find and count the pulse beat in the wrist. The beat that you can count in the wrist comes from a large artery.
2. Let each member of the class count his pulse when sitting in the school room. Now let each member of the class run one hundred feet at his best speed. Then immediately count the pulse to see how many beats the heart has increased from the running. The one whose heart beat has increased least has won in this test.
3. In the same way let each member of the class count the number of times he naturally breathes in one minute while sitting in the school room. Then run the race as before and count the number of breaths in one minute immediately after running. The one whose breathing has increased least and who is least out of breath has won in this test, providing he has run as far and as fast as the others.

CHAPTER XVI

KEEPING THE BODY STRAIGHT

The superintendent of a large business where many boys are employed, tells me that he always picks for the boy who can stand up straight on both feet.

The first thing this superintendent notices is whether the boy who wants a job carries his head up, his shoulders erect and his entire body well poised. He says that a habit of lounging in standing or sitting shows a careless nature and inattention. He will not hire a boy who has a slouchy, shuffling walk.

One of the first things a soldier is taught is to keep the body straight. The shoulders must be back and carried squarely and evenly. The chest must be high, and the head well up with the chin drawn in. We all admire the appearance of the soldier. Why should we not all learn to carry ourselves as straight as soldiers!

The harm of bad postures.—Good posture is as necessary for our health as for our appearance. When one curls down in a chair or leans over a desk with his body bent he is cramping all the organs and crowding them together. Of course this interferes with their work.

First of all, a stooping, cramped posture crowds the lungs. They do not have room to expand, and can no

The kind of "setting up" exercises that train the soldier to be so straight and trim

more take in a full supply of air than a sponge can take in water if you keep it squeezed together.

When the body is bent in a curve the stomach and the liver are cramped and unable to digest the food properly. No doubt many people who think their food

KEEPING THE BODY STRAIGHT

disagrees with them would find that the trouble came from dumping themselves down in a chair in a bad posture after eating.

Good sitting postures.—The chair or desk in which we sit should fit the body. It should be so curved

This outdoor drill will not only rest the boys and girls from their studies, but will teach them to hold their bodies straight and in good posture

as to support the back. It should be of the right height, so that we do not have to sit forward or slide down in the seat to rest the feet on the floor. Then, having the right kind of a seat, we should train ourselves to sit properly.

It is especially important that boys and girls should learn to sit well in school, for they sit so much of the time. And bad habits of posture formed at this time are very hard to break.

When one is at work at a table or desk he should sit well forward. His body should be erect, chest well up, and head in good position. If it is necessary to lean forward toward the desk the body should be bent from the hips, and not curved in the back.

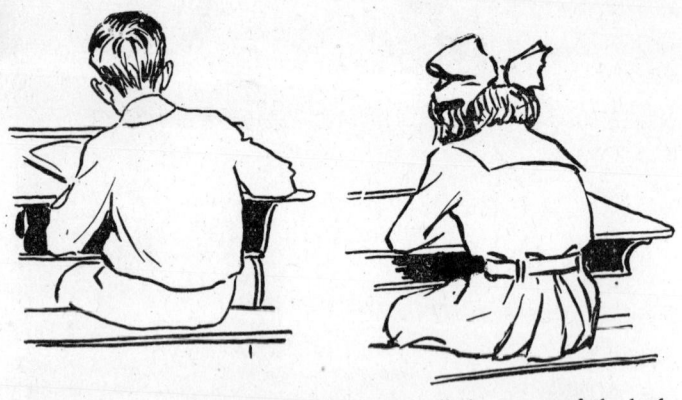

Avoid such postures as these. They cramp all the organs of the body, and result in crooked backs

Crooked backs.—About one out of every five of the boys and girls who study this book have backs or shoulders that are more or less crooked. This trouble is called *curvature of the spine*.

Not all cases of curvature are bad enough that they are easily noticed. Some will have round shoulders. Some will have backbones that crook to one side. Others will have backs that curve in too much.

KEEPING THE BODY STRAIGHT

A part of this difficulty often comes from certain diseases of the bones we have as children. But much of it is caused by our own bad postures.

Habits to avoid.—These are some of the bad

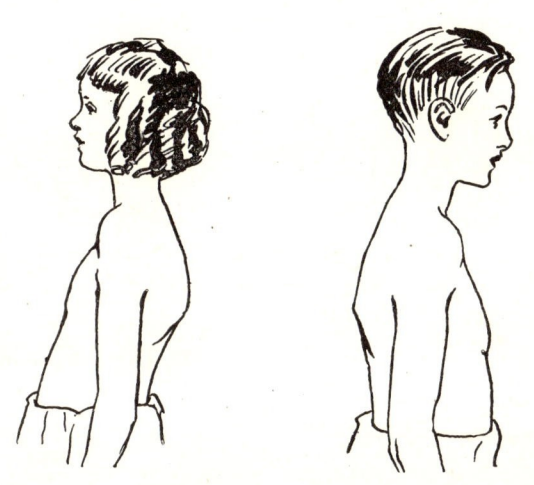

The best way is to be careful not to make our backs crooked by bad postures. Watch your posture and see whether you are making your shoulders round or your spine crooked

habits of posture that may give us crooked backs or shoulders:

1. Standing slouchily, resting the weight on one foot.
2. Sitting and working at a desk which is too high, and which causes one shoulder to be higher than the other.

3. Sitting on one foot, with the body curved to one side.
4. Carrying books or other articles under one arm.
5. Bending forward as we work.

How to stand.—A simple test for good standing posture is this. When one is standing correctly, his body is so balanced that he can rise up on his toes without having to sway the body in the least backward or forward in order to keep his balance. An easy way to learn correct posture is to play at walking a fallen log; the arms extended sidewise will serve as a balance pole; the easy poise this gives may be made a habit.

The wrong way to lie while sleeping. The pillow is too high, and the body bent

It is worth while for all of us to watch our postures and train our bodies to stand and sit erect. No one likes the swagger of the bully, but neither do we admire the slouch of the tramp. Erect, springy carriage usually goes along with a feeling of self-respect. We compliment a person of decision and ability by saying he is "no slouch."

KEEPING THE BODY STRAIGHT

Posture when we sleep.—Our sleeping posture is as important as our waking posture. The mattress should not be too soft, nor should the springs sag. We should train ourselves to lie with the body fully stretched out and not curled up. The pillows should be low, in order that the neck may not be bent and so interfere with the circulation of the blood in the great veins and arteries that pass to the head. Many persons prefer to sleep with no pillow at all. We should sleep on the side rather than on the back or on the face.

The right way to lie while sleeping—pillow **low**, and body straight and relaxed

Interesting things to do.—1. Show how to stand like a soldier on "inspection."
2. Show how to sit properly in a chair for reading.
3. Show how to sit at your school desk when you have writing or studying to do.
4. Draw chalk line on the floor to represent a fallen log; walk the log and keep your balance.
5. Show how to test standing posture by rising up on the toes.

CHAPTER XVII

THE SKIN AND ITS USES

Did you ever meet with an accident and have a piece of skin scraped off? If so, you have discovered one of the most important uses of the skin. This is to protect the delicate and tender nerve endings, millions of which come to the surface of the body, to end in the numberless little organs of touch, temperature and pain, which are in the skin.

Most wonderful of all of the uses of the skin, however, is to serve as a regulator of the heat of the body. The janitor of a school building told me recently that the regulators attached to the heating system of the building were so perfect that the temperature of the school rooms did not vary more than a few degrees throughout the winter.

This is truly wonderful, but the heat of the body is regulated more accurately than that.

How the skin regulates the heat of the body.— You may go out into the heat of the summer sunshine and run or play or work until you are streaming with sweat and feel perfectly roasted. You may stand on a chilly day in the fall and watch a foot-ball game

THE SKIN AND ITS USES

until you feel as if you were half frozen. You may go out skating on the ice when the temperature is twenty degrees below zero, or you may sit quietly in your school room with the room at a temperature of seventy degrees. In spite of all these differences of temperature, your body, if you are well, has not changed its inner temperature by more than the fraction of one degree.

A remarkable experiment.—More than a century ago a number of scientists tried a most interesting and daring experiment. They fixed up a number of rooms so that they could heat them to any degree of temperature that they chose.

Then they first tried going into rooms that were well above 100 degrees of temperature. This was too warm to be comfortable, of course, but they found that they were not injured.

They kept on increasing the heat of their rooms until they were living and breathing in a room so hot that you would suppose they would die. But the air, being dry and quiet, did not injure them.

Now we often put sore joints into a box and then heat the air in the box to the boiling point and over. But the joint is not injured; it is helped. Of course, the living tissue of the joint does not get as hot as the air around it. It would die if it did. It is protected by a layer of quiet air next to the skin, which the skin is able in a remarkable manner to keep cooled down.

We learned in an earlier chapter, as you will remember, that the body can not change its inner temperature more than a few degrees without the most serious consequences.

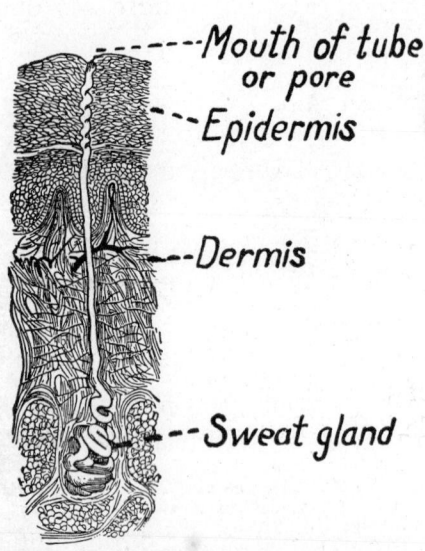

This wonderful regulation of temperature is brought about by the skin. To understand how the skin works, it will be necessary to know something of its structure.

The structure of the skin.—The skin is about as thick as the leather in the upper of your shoe. It consists of two layers. There is first an outer, hard, tough layer called the *epidermis*, which is made of scaly cells which are not sensible to pain and which do not bleed when scraped or cut. These outer cells are constantly falling and rubbing off. They form in little rolls when you rub the skin after a bath. They also form the dandruff in your hair. Next there is an inner layer called the *dermis*, which

This drawing shows a section of the skin, very much magnified, with a sweat gland and its tube leading to the surface. The sweat glands are so close together that the skin contains many millions of them

THE SKIN AND ITS USES

contains many nerves and blood-vessels. When this layer of the skin is cut or torn it causes pain and bleeding.

Opening outward on every portion of the skin are millions of little mouths or wells called pores. These lead by a tiny spiral tube down through the skin, where they end in a little knob or gland. These are the sweat glands and their openings. Now let us see how the sweat glands work.

When the weather is not warm, or when the body is not heated up by exercise, the sweat glands may not send out more than a pint of moisture to be evaporated; but when the body is greatly heated they may supply enough to fill the gallon measure

The pores and sweat glands.—When the body becomes heated by exercise or from being in too high a temperature, a watery fluid called *perspiration* is gathered by these glands and poured out through their numberless little tubes upon the surface of the skin. We then say that the person is sweating or perspiring. The perspiration immediately begins to evaporate from the skin. It is the evaporating of the perspiration that cools the body when it becomes too heated.

The amount of sweat given out in a day by an adult may vary from one pint to at least a gallon, depending upon the temperature in which the person works.

When the body becomes cold the pores close and the perspiration is checked. The heat of the body then rises.

If anything happens to interfere with the regulation of the body's heat, the temperature rises and we then have a fever.

We must remember that these sweat glands are constantly at work, even when we do not know that we are perspiring. Because of this the skin is always somewhat moist.

Evaporation cools the body.—It is the evaporation of this moisture on the skin that makes it easy to take cold if one sits down in a draft. For when moving air passes rapidly over the moist skin, the evaporation is very rapid, and the cooling is therefore quick.

When the skin is suddenly cooled, the blood is driven away from the surface of the body. It thereupon is forced to some other part of the body, as the throat or nose, and congests the blood-vessels by overcrowding. This is not the whole story, for there often are germs in our nose waiting for just such an opportunity as this to inflame the nose.

It is this congestion of the blood-vessels which gives us the feeling of stuffiness in our nose and throat when a cold begins.

To prevent colds one should therefore keep the body from cooling too rapidly, especially if the skin is moist

THE SKIN AND ITS USES

from excessive perspiration. This means that we should avoid sitting in drafts when we are heated.

Driving away a cold.—If we feel a cold coming on, the remedy is to draw the blood away from the place where it is becoming congested. To do this we should rest in a room where the air is fresh. We may then take a hot bath, soak the feet in hot water, drink hot liquids, like lemonade, and cover up warmly in bed.

Questions to answer.—1. Why does the doctor put his thermometer under your tongue to see how sick you are? How many degrees should the thermometer show if you are well? About what is your temperature if you have a slight fever? If you have a high fever?

2. Suppose after you have been out playing until you are very warm you come into the house and find a cool breeze blowing in through an open window. Should you sit down in the breeze to cool off? Why?

3. What are the signs by which you can tell a cold coming on? Does your throat get sore? Does your head feel stopped up? Do you get hoarse? Do your lungs feel tight? Does your head ache? Tell what you can do, when a cold threatens, in order to drive it away.

4. Georgia has a sore throat and is coughing badly, but wants to go to school. What do you advise about it?

CHAPTER XVIII

KEEPING CLEAN

One of the first and I suppose best reasons for keeping clean is that it is more or less of a disgrace to be dirty.

Of course one may get his hands much soiled and his body covered with dust and dirt in his play or his work. But nobody minds fresh dirt which is washed off as soon as possible. It is the dirt that is left on that is repulsive.

If we have dirty hands and face, unwashed and uncombed hair, a body that needs a bath but does not get it, these are telltale signs to every one about us that we lack something of neatness and good breeding.

Keeping the pores open.—But there is another important reason why the skin should be kept clean. This is to keep the pores open. We learned in the last chapter how the glands of the skin regulate the heat of the body by the sweat they pour out on the surface of the skin. The sweat is chiefly water, but it also contains a certain amount of solid waste matter from the tissues.

An average of perhaps two or three teaspoonfuls of this waste is thrown out through the pores each day.

KEEPING CLEAN

The solid matter unites with an oily substance that comes from small glands at the roots of the hairs which cover most of the body. This mixture sticks to the skin, and clogs up the mouths of the pores.

When the pores are clogged the sending out of perspiration is interfered with and the proper regulation of the body's heat is impossible. The waste matter and oil soon grow stale on the skin if they are not removed and come to have an unpleasant odor. And who wants to offend others by the odors from his body!

Good bathing habits.—The body should be thoroughly washed with warm water and soap about twice a week. Many persons take a bath every day. This is a good habit to form, though it is not necessary that hot water baths shall be taken so frequently.

For those who are well and vigorous a good rule is

Every really *clean* boy and girl desires to start each day with a good wash for hands and face, and to take a bath often enough to keep the skin fresh and clean to take a cold sponge or shower every morning, and a hot bath once or twice a week. Since hot baths cause us to relax and get sleepy, they should be taken at night when we are ready for bed. The cold bath awakens and invigorates, so it should be taken in the morning.

Some people do not like cold baths. They shiver and shrink at the very idea. Now no one should take a cold bath if it leaves him cold and chilly afterward. There must be a reaction and glow over the skin if the cold bath is to have a good effect.

Learning to enjoy cold baths.—But one who shrinks from cold water can usually train the skin by starting with moderately cool water, and then going on from day to day with water a few degrees colder. It is well to start with a temperature of about 80 degrees. The training may go on until the shock is not too great with water at 50 degrees.

A good way to take a cold bath at first is to stand in a tub of warm water up nearly to the knees. Then sponge the body with water as cold as can be endured without too much chilling. As soon as the sponging is finished step out of the tub and rub the body with a coarse towel until a glow is produced and the body feels warm. After a few days of this practise, a strong, healthy person may shower or pour the cold water over the body instead of using the sponge. The cold bath should always be taken in a warm room, and should occupy only a few minutes.

KEEPING CLEAN

Training the skin against taking colds.—If we get our skin trained to cold water bathing, it will do much to insure against taking cold. The wearing of loose porous clothing which allows a free air bath of the skin as we go about our work or play will also do much to toughen the skin against colds.

The skin of the face and hands may get rough, chap, and even crack open from exposure to cold winds. The hands will also chap from getting them wet in the snow. To prevent chapping, the skin may be rubbed before going out with glycerine, vaseline or with rose water. Chapping may be cured by bathing the skin in soft, warm water, drying carefully, and then rubbing with any good oil or face cream.

The important points to remember about the skin.—After the perspiration has evaporated the waste matter and oil from the hair roots remain on the skin. These clog the pores and give off a bad odor, which tells everybody that we need a bath.

When the skin is not kept clean it can no longer regulate the heat of the body. We are then liable to colds and other dangers to our health. The only way to keep the skin clean is by frequent bathing.

The skin can be trained to enjoy a cold bath or the contact of cool air. Training of the skin in this way is one of the best safe-guards against taking cold.

HYGIENE AND HEALTH

Very rapid cooling of the skin when we are perspiring is always dangerous, and we should never run the risk of drafts when we are heated.

Good habits to form.—1. The habit of taking a cold shower or sponge every morning as a protection against colds and as a matter of cleanliness.

2. The habit of taking a warm bath with plenty of soap and rubbing just before going to bed at least once a week; twice is better. If the warm bath is taken during the day it should be followed with a dash of cold water.

3. Wearing the very lightest clothing in the morning while brushing the teeth, combing the hair or performing other tasks about our room. This will train the skin to changes of temperature.

Health Problems

1. Make a list of the health "friend-habits" you have formed.
2. The day was warm and Harold had played hard and grown rather sweaty. He was tired and sleepy when he prepared for bed, so he dumped his clothes in a pile on the floor. In the morning they were damp and did not smell fresh. Can you give the rules Harold should follow about his clothes when he prepares for bed?
3. Do you follow the rules you have given for the care of the clothes when you prepare for bed?

CHAPTER XIX

CLOTHING AND ITS CARE

Long ago, in the time before there were civilized nations or great cities, people wore very little clothing. In warm countries there were to be found many tribes who wore almost no clothes at all. And even yet there are to be found primitive peoples whose customs permit them to go about with the body but partly covered.

With us clothing has become a very important matter. Everybody likes to be neat and well-dressed. The person who goes with ragged or dirty clothes is very unfortunate and to be pitied.

Materials for our clothing.—Four great materials go into the making of the fabric for our clothing: *cotton* from the fields of the sunny South and other warm countries; *wool* from the backs of the sheep; *linen* from the fiber of the flax; and *silk* spun by the silk worm. The producing of these materials and making them up into clothing is one of our greatest industries.

Making our clothing look well.—There are certain rules which must be followed if our clothes are to look well.

1. Our clothes must be planned for the use we desire of them. When our work is rough and heavy our clothes must be of heavy, strong material, and be plainly made. Our school clothes should be of strong, durable material which is easily made clean. Our best clothes may be of finer material, and more attractively made.
2. In order to be attractive, our clothes must fit us. They must not be too large nor too small, nor look as if they had been planned for some one else.
3. No clothing, no matter how fine, looks well if it is not properly cared for. Clothes should be kept neat and clean with no rips nor places that need patching, and with no missing buttons.

Four things required of clothing.—Besides making our clothing attractive, there are four other things to have in mind in planning our dress. These are:

1. Proper ventilation of the skin.
2. Reasonable warmth.
3. Cleanliness.
4. Freedom from pressure or binding.

We learned in an earlier lesson the important part the skin plays in regulating the heat of the body and helping the body get rid of waste material. Our clothes should be of such fabrics as will allow the air to come freely to the skin, and at the same time keep it warm.

CLOTHING AND ITS CARE

The right kind of cloth.—Cloth that is loose and porous will allow the air to pass through much more readily than cloth that is hard and close woven. Underwear should therefore always be of a porous kind of cloth. The outer clothing also is better when it is made of cloth having a loose weave rather than a hard, glazed material. Even the linings of coats and vests should be of porous cloth.

It is necessary when we are out in a heavy rain to wear a rubber coat if we would keep dry. But one soon feels the discomfort from a rubber coat, even on a cool day. The skin can not get a supply of fresh air through the rubber, and the entire body suffers from its lack.

The warmth of clothing.—The amount of clothing we wear should be regulated by the coldness of the weather and the amount of exercise we are taking. While one should wear clothing enough to be comfortable, it is always a mistake to wear thicker clothing than we need. This is because heavy clothing does not allow the ventilation of the body as easily as thinner clothing.

Woolens protect against the cold better than any other fabric since woolen cloth has many air spaces among its fibers. And these air spaces are poor conductors of heat, and therefore do not allow the body to cool off readily. Clothing of light color is somewhat cooler in summer and warmer in winter than dark clothing.

Woolen and cotton clothing.—Some prefer underwear of wool, some of cotton, some linen, others silk, while still others mixtures of two or three of these fabrics. It really makes little difference which we choose after we get used to one. The important thing is that our underwear be very porous, since it is not so much the material as the layer of air it encloses which keeps us warm. For that reason a coarse webbing like a fisherman's net is very satisfactory.

Woolen outside garments make the best protection against the winter's cold

For sick persons woolen underwear is, on the whole, the best. It will keep dry longest, and when moist chills the skin less. The great objection to wool is that we all prefer thin underwear, since our houses are warm and we don our overcoats when we go outdoors, but a thin woolen garment is expensive and easily ruined in the laundry.

CLOTHING AND ITS CARE

Keeping our clothing clean.—Our clothing should be kept clean, first of all, because nobody likes to see one in dirty garments. One's under-garments quickly become soiled from the perspiration and waste matter of the skin, and should be changed at least twice a week.

The outer garments should, as far as possible, be of goods that can be washed. If it is necessary to wear a fabric that can not be washed, it should be thoroughly sponged or dry cleaned often enough that it may also be fresh and free from dirt.

No piece of clothing on any part of the body should be tight enough to bind. This is because an important part of the circulation of the blood is carried on immediately beneath the skin.

Why our clothes should not be tight.—Tight belts, neckwear, garters, or other clothing, hinder this circulation, and also may interfere somewhat with the flow of blood in the deeper veins. Especially should one not wear tight bands around the neck to interfere with the flow of blood from the brain. Hats which bind tightly on the head also interfere with the circulation of blood in the scalp, and this may prove an injury to the hair.

Tight shoes which interfere with the circulation of blood in the feet not only produce corns, but tend to keep one's feet cold in cold weather. They also prevent the proper development of the feet, and weaken them. Low shoes and sandals are better than high shoes, since they allow the air to come more freely to the feet.

Habits worth forming about our clothing:—

1. Having a reasonable pride in our clothes, so we shall always desire to be neat, clean attractive.
2. Using care not to soil or wear out our clothes more than is necessary.
3. Keeping our clothes well brushed, spots sponged off, and worn places repaired.
4. Keeping our clothes carefully hung up or laid away when we are not wearing them, so that they will not get soiled and wrinkled.

Health Problems

1. Look your clothing over to see whether there are spots that ought to be removed.
2. Give directions (ask your mother) for removing grease spots; fruit stains; ink stains.
3. Discover how many different kinds of materials (wool, cotton, etc.) are represented in the clothing you are now wearing. Tell how each is grown or produced.
4. Do you think it is a good plan for one to begin in the fall to bundle the throat up with wraps?
5. What "clothing habits" ought children to form? Make a list of ten such habits.

CHAPTER XX

WHEN WE PLAY

After work then play! All the really fine, promising boys and girls I know like to play. I think all of them like to work, too. At least it is much more fun to play when one has done his work, so that he has earned the right to play.

Years ago most people thought that time spent in play was wasted. In the New England Primer, which was used as a reading book when your great grandparents went to school, children are urged to "mind little play." After their work was done I suppose they were expected to sit solemn and "be good"!

Now we know that just as every one ought to work, so ought every one to play. For play quickens the heart beat, makes us breathe deep and strong, and helps in many ways to health and growth.

Why we play.—While play is good for the health, one does not want of course to think about his health while playing. We play best and get the most good out of it when we play for the fun of playing. We play to develop skill and become expert in games. And we also play to win in the game when we can win fairly.

It is worth while to know how to play. One never likes to have to say, "I don't know how to play that game," or "I can not play that well." We should not be satisfied to know how to play just a few games, but should learn as many as possible of the plays and games suitable to our age.

Indian Club Race

Three clubs are stood upright in a small circle. The runner starts from a point thirty feet away, runs and moves one of the clubs to an adjoining circle, and returns to the starting point; she makes one trip for each of the three clubs. The one who can move all three clubs in the shortest time has won the game

Rules we must learn.—There are certain rules which coaches and trainers of athletes always insist upon, and which every one should follow.

1. Break in to hard playing gradually so as **not** to over-tax the strength.

WHEN WE PLAY

2. Play only in air that is pure and free from dust.
3. Do not play hard just before or just after eating.
4. Take a bath after finishing a game.
5. Always be fair and square in a game, never cheating nor taking unfair advantage of an opponent.

When the foot-ball team starts work in the fall or the runners begin to train for the track meet, the coach requires that they break in gradually. They do not try full speed at first, for this would keep them from reaching their full strength.

When one plays he breathes very much more air into the lungs than when he is still. It is therefore important that the air he breathes should be free from dust and impurities. We should play out-of-doors on the grass or clean play-ground whenever possible.

Good air where we play.—We can hardly do a worse thing than to play in a room where the air is bad or where dust rises from the floor as we play. Not only will playing in this kind of place keep us from getting any advantage from the playing, but it may very seriously endanger our health. When we are forced to play inside, as in a gymnasium or play-room, we should see that the floor is very clean and free from dust and that the windows are wide open, so that plenty of fresh air may enter.

HYGIENE AND HEALTH

I know a boy who is fine in his play and games. He can outrun and outjump most other boys of his age. But for several nights past when he has come in to supper from play he has not been hungry. When his mother asked him about his appetite, he said, "Oh, I guess I played too hard, that is all."

Getting fresh air and sunshine while at play

Playing hard just before meals.—It is possible to play too hard just before meals and to become so excited and wrought up that we lose our appetite because of the strain of the play. If the play is hard and tiring, one should quit his play at least half an hour before meal-time. He should then sit down or lie

WHEN WE PLAY

down and rest before eating. If he does not do this, he will find that he is not quite so good in his plays after a time. His growth will not go on quite as fast as it should, and he will not be as strong as he would like to be. A good athlete must be a good eater.

Nor should one play too soon after eating. When one has eaten a full meal the blood flows to the stomach to enable it to carry on its digestion of the food. Now if one goes immediately to play as soon as he has finished his meal, the muscles and skin call for the blood. The stomach is robbed of its proper supply. It is plain that the digestion of our food can not go on so well under these conditions.

Playing after eating.—There is another reason why we should not play exciting games too soon after eating. Some experiments recently performed upon cats show that if the cat is excited or irritated soon after eating, the food does not digest as it should. Excitement hinders digestion. We should give both body and mind a brief rest after eating.

After athletes have been in a game, they always come in and immediately take a bath. We should do exactly the same way, for the activity of play increases our perspiration and the amount of waste matter brought to the surface of the skin.

The bath following the game.—Usually the body gathers more or less dust in the course of playing, and this mixes with the sweat and waste of the skin. This greasy dirt coating must be washed off in order to give the skin the chance to do its work properly.

Another good reason for bathing after playing is that everybody wants to feel that he is clean and neat all the time. He can not feel this way unless he has cleaned up after his play.

Interesting things to do.—1. Have a contest in the class to see who can write down the longest list of the names of plays and games.
2. Write down the names of all the games and plays you know how to play. Which are suitable for indoor and which for outdoor playing?
3. Lay off a running track of 100 feet along one side of the play-ground. Then have races and time the different runners with a watch that has a second hand.
4. Plan contests of broad jumping, high jumping, chinning the bar, etc. Dig up with a spade a soft place to light on in the jumping. In jumping matches, athletes never light on hard ground, as the jar injures them.

Health Problems

1. Margery complained that the girls did not want her to play with them. The girls said that Margery never would play what the rest wanted, but always insisted on playing what she liked best. What would you advise Margery to do about it?
2. Report on Health Crusader habits.

CHAPTER XXI

SLEEP, REST AND DREAMS

If there is a baby at your house, you have **probably** noticed that about every time you go to look at it, it is asleep. For the first year of its life the baby should sleep about sixteen hours out of every twenty-four.

By the time you were two years old you had slept a year and a half. When you were ten years old you had slept about six years. When you are twenty you will have slept ten years. Taking our life-time through, we average sleeping fully one-third of the time.

The importance of sleep.—Sleep is so important that no one can live beyond four or five days without sleeping. Soldiers who are kept many hours without sleep, as in a battle, often get so sleepy that they will fall asleep with the shells bursting around them.

It is said that when in olden times cruel jailers wished to torment prisoners, they would do this by keeping them awake for several days at a time. This is one of the most cruel punishments that could be invented.

If you want to grow rapidly and be well and strong, you must make sure of plenty of good unbroken sleep. Children from ten to twelve years of age should have at least ten hours of sleep, and some may require as much as eleven.

Regular habits about sleeping.—One should have a regular time to go to bed, and not go early one night and late the next. One reason for this is that we can train ourselves to become sleepy at a certain time and then go to sleep much more quickly when we go to bed than if we do not have any certain time for retiring.

Our bed-time should be reasonably early, so that we may arise early in the morning. If we get up late we usually have to hurry with our breakfast in order to get away to school in time.

Good sleep and good nature go together.—Have you ever noticed that some mornings you get up happy and cheerful, and everything seems pleasant? Another morning you may awaken cross and tired, and everything you touch goes wrong. Your good mornings always follow a good night of sleep, and your bad mornings a night when your sleep was not restful, or when you did not have enough.

It has been found by careful experiments that one sleeps much more soundly the first one or two hours after he gets to sleep than he does later in the night. And yet this first sleep would seem to be no more restful than sleep in the later part of the sleep period.

We often dream when we are asleep, and no doubt you have often wondered at the queer things that come into your dreams.

SLEEP, REST AND DREAMS

Dreams.—We will understand dreams better if we remember that they are nothing but *sleep thinking*. When we are asleep there is nothing to control the current of our thoughts as there is when we are awake, so they run off in many strange directions and play us queer tricks. Most of our dreams do not matter, but sometimes we have dreams that frighten us and disturb our sleep.

Bad dreams are sometimes caused by indigestion coming from heavy suppers, or from eating indigestible things just before going to bed. It is thought that "nightmares" may also be caused by lying in cramped positions when we are asleep, and in this way interfering with certain blood-vessels.

Whenever possible, we should sleep alone, and not with some other person in the bed. If two must sleep in the same room, each should have his own bed.

Fresh air while we sleep.—It is fully as important that we should have plenty of fresh air when we are asleep as when we are awake. We sleep more soundly and rest better in fresh air. We should have the windows of our sleeping rooms open all night, either in the summer-time or in the winter. When it is very cold we should put extra covering on the bed, but not shut out the air.

Many people who keep their windows open in the summer, close them tight in the winter. They seem to think that because the air is so cold it is certainly pure. We are to remember that air becomes impure when it is cold in the winter just as when it is hot in the summer.

Sleeping out-of-doors.—The very best way of all is to sleep out-of-doors on a sleeping porch, where the air can freely enter and pass over our beds all night. We are told that tuberculosis was practically

Rest after play

unknown in the world until people began to live in tightly closed houses. Wise physicians who treat patients for tuberculosis have them sleep out-of-doors in this way. And surely if this is good for sick persons, it is equally good for those who are well.

It has been noticed that pneumonia is worse in February and March than at any other time of the year.

This is not because these months are really worse than any other months. It is because they come at the end of the winter, when many people who have

SLEEP, REST AND DREAMS

slept in tightly closed bedrooms all winter fall easy prey to the pneumonia germs after their strength has been lowered by sleeping in impure air.

Good sleep habits to form.—1. Going to bed regularly and getting up regularly, making sure of plenty of sleep.

2. Going to sleep promptly as soon as we get to bed, not stopping to talk with any one who may sleep with us.

3. Getting up as soon as we waken or are called, and not waiting to drowse after we have had sleep enough.

4. Lying in a comfortable, straight position on the side.

5. Sleeping out-of-doors if possible; if not, with open windows every night in the year.

Health Problems

1. Do you ever have bad dreams, or nightmares? Do you have trouble to get to sleep? If so, can you discover the cause: Do you eat food for supper or before going to bed which does not agree with you? Do you read exciting, blood-curdling stories in the evening? Do you play hard up to time to go to bed?

2. Josephine objects to going to bed at the proper time in the evening and then is sleepy and tired when it is time to get up. What would you advise?

CHAPTER XXII

THE TEETH

Whenever one laughs or smiles or talks he displays his teeth to every one who may be looking at him. No part of the face is more attractive than a set of clean, regular, white and shiny teeth.

But, on the other hand, nothing is much more ugly than teeth that are stained and slimy with decayed food, or that are crooked, deformed, or decayed in the mouth.

When we get our teeth.—The baby at first has no teeth, but by the time it is a year old four teeth have appeared in front in the upper jaw and four in the lower jaw. So, on the baby's first birthday he should have eight teeth.

During the second year three more come immediately back of these first ones on each side of the jaw. This adds six teeth for each jaw, or twelve in all during the second year. These, with the eight that grew in the first year, make twenty teeth that the child should have when it is two years old.

These twenty teeth are called milk teeth, since they appear while the child is so young that its food is still

THE TEETH

chiefly of milk. The twenty milk teeth are all lost between the age of seven and ten years. They become loose and are pushed out by the new second, or permanent, teeth which are growing in to take their place.

The first permanent teeth.—At the age of about six years the first of the permanent teeth appear. These are known as the sixth year molars. One sixth year molar comes in on each side of the jaw just back of the last milk tooth. There are four sixth year molars in all, two in each jaw.

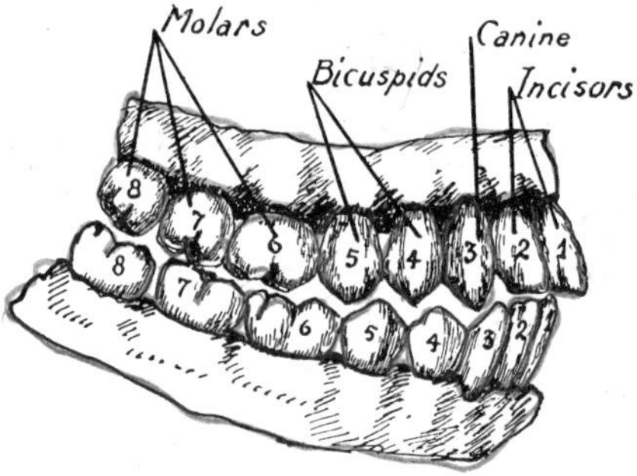

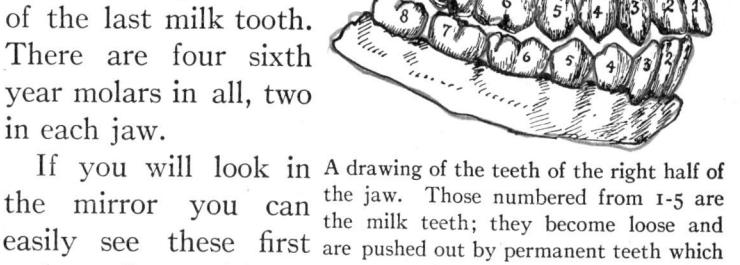

If you will look in the mirror you can easily see these first molars. Start with the first tooth to the right or the left side of the middle, and count around to the sixth tooth. This is the first of your permanent teeth, and is the sixth year molar. This tooth is numbered 6 in the picture.

A drawing of the teeth of the right half of the jaw. Those numbered from 1-5 are the milk teeth; they become loose and are pushed out by permanent teeth which come to take their place. Those numbered 6 are the first permanent teeth to appear

Let us stop now and count up how many teeth one should have at the age of eleven years. First of all there are the twenty permanent teeth which have taken the place of the twenty milk teeth at different times between the ages of seven and ten years. Then there are the four sixth year molars, the very first of one's permanent teeth. This makes twenty-four.

A complete set of teeth.—Every boy and girl at the age of eleven ought, therefore, to have twenty-four straight, sound, white teeth. Four additional molars will come in during the next year or two (number 7 in the picture), making twenty-eight altogether. And finally, probably sometime between the age of seventeen and twenty years, four more molars, called *wisdom teeth*, appear. This makes the complete set of thirty-two teeth.

Yesterday as I was going down town on the car I sat beside a pretty schoolgirl friend, who told me she was on her way to the dentist. She is very much concerned because her teeth are so crooked that they altogether spoil the appearance of her mouth. She is having the dentist try to straighten them for her.

Why some teeth come in crooked.—This girl told me the way her teeth happened to grow crooked. When her second teeth were coming in, the milk teeth did not become loose and come out properly. She neglected to have the dentist look after them, and some of the second teeth grew out of the side of the gum instead of coming in where the first tooth had been. The dentist can help her even now, but it would have been much better had she gone to him when her permanent teeth were coming in.

THE TEETH

Not only do crooked teeth look unsightly, but they do not fit together right when we chew. In this way they make it impossible to cut and grind the food properly. This results in food being swallowed without good mastication, and the stomach has much harder work to digest it.

Protecting teeth from decay.—The greatest enemy of our teeth is decay. School physicians tell us that at least nine school children out of every ten have one or more teeth with cavities in them caused by decay. When we remember that the teeth we have at eleven or twelve years must last us all through our lives, we see how important it is that we shall keep them sound.

Injury from decayed teeth.—Decayed teeth are certain to attack the health of the entire body. There are four different ways in which decayed teeth injure us.

1. They make it impossible to chew the food properly. Food which is not well chewed not only goes to the stomach in chunks that are too large, but it fails to be properly mixed with the saliva in the mouth.
2. The cavity of a decayed tooth discharges poisons into the mouth. These are swallowed and taken up by the blood and carried all over the body.

3. Besides these poisons, decaying teeth cause toothache. Sound teeth never ache.

4. Every cavity in a tooth is filled with a mixture of decayed food and microbes. More than 100 different kinds of microbes have been found in the mouth. Many of these are the germs of serious diseases like tuberculosis and diphtheria. We will see in the next lesson how to keep our teeth from decaying.

Interesting things to do.—1. Learn from the drawing on page 145 the four different names that apply to your teeth.

2. Point to each tooth in the right or left half of either jaw and as you point to it give it its name.

3. After learning the age at which the different teeth usually come in, point again to each of your different teeth and tell the age at which this tooth usually appears.

4. Report whether you have ever had the toothache, whether you have been to the dentist, and how many, if any, teeth you have had filled.

5. Examine your teeth carefully after cleaning them to see whether you can find any cavities. Use a toothpick to explore around the teeth.

6. Play you are a dentist: First scrub your hands very clean, then examine the teeth of a classmate and give directions for caring for the teeth.

CHAPTER XXIII

HOW TO HAVE GOOD TEETH

A doctor who had examined the mouths of a large number of school children kept a record of the troubles he found with their teeth. He says:

"The average school child has twenty-four teeth; eight of them are diseased; sixteen of them are discolored with unsightly accumulation of foods and deposits, or else he has some noticeable malformation interfering with mastication. Three of the four sixth year molars are seriously affected, or else one is already lost and another decayed. He has had toothache more or less during the past year. He has never put a toothbrush to his teeth and has never seen the inside of a dentist's office."

Learning to care for our teeth.—This description, severe as it is, is true of about one-half of the children in the schools. Most of this trouble can be saved by keeping our teeth strong by eating coarse food and by forming right habits of caring for them when we are young.

The cause of most of our tooth troubles is decay. Decay, as we have already learned, is caused by

HYGIENE AND HEALTH

microbes. If we keep our mouths free from microbes, then our teeth will be safe from decay.

Microbes are attracted to our mouths by the particles of food that remain sticking to our teeth. Clean mouths mean fewer microbes. If we clean our teeth

My mother taught me to use a tooth-brush

I wish mine had

thoroughly two or three times a day, we will get rid of most of the microbes that cause our teeth to decay. There is no other way to have good teeth.

The tooth-brush habit.—The first thing to do if we would have clean teeth is to get a tooth-brush. The next thing to do is to *use* the tooth-brush faithfully! For not everybody who owns a tooth-brush uses it regularly.

HOW TO HAVE GOOD TEETH

Our tooth-brush should have bristles stiff enough so they will push well into the angles of the teeth. The bristles should not be so stiff, however, as to hurt the gums. The bristles should not be set too close together, for this will keep them from going in between the teeth.

Besides a good tooth-brush, we need a tooth paste or powder. This is to help dissolve and cut the slime from the teeth. The paste or powder should be used each morning, and may be used also in the evening. It is well also to brush the teeth with clear water after the noon meal, but they should always be brushed at least morning and evening. If our teeth are cleaned thoroughly this often, the microbes will not have a chance to stay long enough in our mouths to cause decay.

How to use a tooth-brush.—Not everybody knows how to use a tooth-brush. I watched my nephew brush his teeth this morning, and he just rubbed the brush back and forth over them. This did not get the bristles into the corners between the teeth. Besides brushing back and forth, he needs to give the brush a twisting movement, or else work the brush downward for the upper teeth and upward for the lower teeth. In this way the bristles get into every crack and corner.

Teeth nearly always begin to decay at their inner edge where they touch each other. This is because

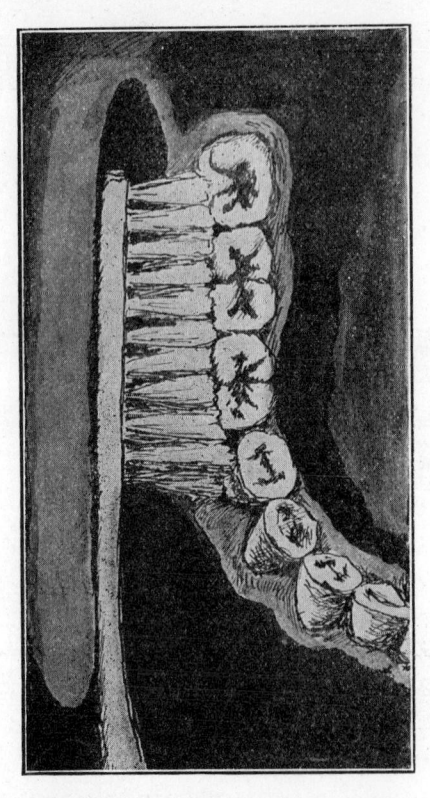

A tooth-brush with tufts of bristles of slightly different lengths is better than one with bristles all the same length; this is because the longer bristles can then reach in between the teeth better

the food particles are not removed from between the teeth, and when the food begins to decay it also starts the tooth to decay.

Cleaning between the teeth.—To overcome this difficulty, one must clean between the teeth. This can be done by drawing a piece of thread between all the teeth that are far enough apart for the thread to go between them. A special silk thread called *silk floss* is made for this use. It should be used each night when we are getting ready for bed.

No matter how well we care for our teeth, we should call on the dentist at least twice a year and let him look them over. It is possible that some little place has started to decay and needs immediate attention. If the den-

HOW TO HAVE GOOD TEETH

tist discovers the decaying place in time, it will cause no pain to fix it, and the tooth may be made almost as good as ever.

Going to see the dentist.—When a tooth has decayed so much that it begins to ache, it can then never be made as good again as if it had been looked after in time. An aching tooth means that the cavity has got down near to a nerve, and that there will be some pain in cleaning the hole out and filling it. But every brave boy and girl will be willing to stand a little pain in order to have their teeth made good.

Danger of breaking the teeth.—I saw a boy doing a very foolish thing the other day. He was cracking hazel-nuts with his teeth. He probably did not know that the outer part of the tooth, which is called the *enamel*, is very hard and brittle. Because it is so hard the enamel is easily cracked or chipped by biting upon hard substances.

When the enamel has been broken or chipped in any way, the tooth will decay very much more easily and quickly. It is like the apple or potato with the skin broken through—the microbes find a good place for lodgment and immediately begin their work.

Good habits to form.—1. Having as much pride in clean, attractive teeth as we have in good clothes, or clean hands and face. This means that we should be ashamed of dirty, discolored teeth, or of teeth that have cavities in them.

2. Being so faithful in the use of our tooth-brush each night and morning that we would no more think of going without brushing our teeth than we would of going without our breakfast or supper.
3. Making a visit to the dentist at a certain time each year. This might be on our birthday and half way in between.

Interesting things to do.—1. Show how to brush the teeth with a back and forth, up and down and twisting motion so as to get the brush into every crevice between the teeth.
2. Show how to pass a silk thread in between the teeth to remove all particles of food.
3. Show how to apply tooth paste or powder to the brush without waste.

Health Problems

1. Many persons who *own* a tooth-brush do not *use* it regularly. How many times have you brushed your teeth in the last week?
2. Unless a tooth-brush is well washed out after it has been used, it becomes very dirty and not fit to put into one's mouth. Tell how you clean your brush.
3. When did you have toothache last? What caused it? When did you last go to the dentist? When should you go again?

CHAPTER XXIV

CARE OF THE HAIR

Hair grows on nearly all parts of the body. It is longest and thickest, however, on the head, where it serves for protection and adds much to one's appearance.

Hair, bulb, gland.—Each separate hair grows from its own tiny bulb or root which is imbedded in the skin. Pull a hair from your head and draw it through between your finger and thumb. Do you feel the small bulb at the end? Every hair also has its own little oil gland and sometimes two of them, which open directly against the root of the hair. This oiling system supplies all the oil the hair needs and will keep it soft and glossy if the skin from which the hair grows is properly cared for.

Our hair shows the kind of care it gets.—The other day I sat beside a boy in the street-car who would have had a fine head of hair, except that something was the matter with it. His coat collar was covered with little whitish flakes of dandruff and loose hairs that had fallen off of his head.

When this boy raised his cap to his teacher, who came into the car, I noticed that his scalp looked rough and scaly where his hair was parted. He also scratched and rubbed his head now and then as if it was itching or felt uncomfortable.

Now I think I know what was the matter with this boy's head. I think he did not take good care of his hair. Perhaps he had not formed the habit of brushing it and washing it as often as he should.

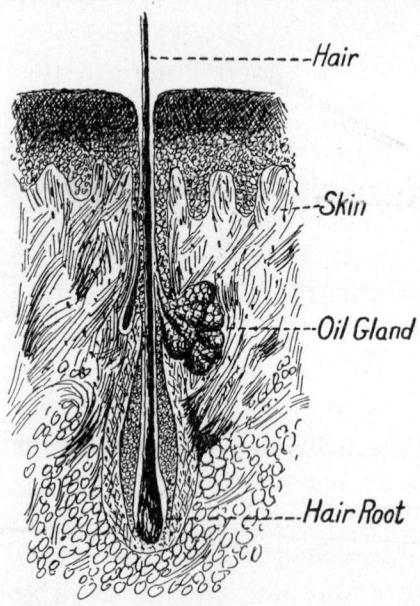

A hair, with its bulb or root, and an oil gland

What dandruff is.—Did you ever think what dandruff really is? Secure a few pieces of dandruff from your hair. Examine them carefully through the magnifying-glass if you have one. If not, your eyes will do. You will find that the little dandruff flakes are nothing but particles of the epidermis that scale off from the scalp.

We have already learned that the epidermis is constantly wearing off. Particles of it loosen and scale

CARE OF THE HAIR

off on all parts of the body. You can sometimes notice the whitish particles in your stockings if you have worn them several days. When the flakes scale off on the scalp they lodge in the hair. They are just like the flakes that scale off on other parts of the body.

Removing dandruff.—It is perfectly natural that everybody should have some dandruff gather in his hair. The trouble is that some have too much. If the head is kept clean and healthy by frequent washing, and the hair is brushed well every day, one will have no trouble with dandruff. It will be removed as fast as it forms, and will not be noticeable. The oil from the glands at the roots of the hair gradually works out to the surface of the scalp. This oily substance is somewhat sticky and mixed with the dandruff forms into a kind of pasty coating. When this dries it sticks to the scalp and finally peals off in scales.

When this sticky mass clings to the scalp, it irritates the skin and makes it feel dry and itchy. This condition is bad for the roots of the hair and causes it to loosen and fall out. Failure to take care of one's hair is a frequent cause of baldness.

Washing the hair.—In order to keep the scalp and hair clean the head should be washed about once a week; twice a week is better if we play or work in the dust or dirt. A mild soap should be used with plenty of warm, soft water. It is safer not to use the prepared shampoo mixtures, for the doctors tell us that many of them are bad for the scalp. After the washing is finished, the soap should be thoroughly rinsed out of the hair. The hair should then be dried carefully before we expose ourselves to draft or the cold.

In order to keep the hair in good condition it should be thoroughly brushed every day. Brushing starts the oil to flowing from the roots of the hair, and gives the hair a glossy, healthy appearance. It is well to massage the scalp with the finger-tips or even to pinch it lightly over the entire surface once or twice a day if we find the hair becoming dry. This will not only cause the oil to come out upon the hair, but will bring more blood to the surface and cause the hair to grow better.

Insects that get into the hair.—Those who do not live in very clean homes or who fail to keep their heads clean are sometimes troubled with small head lice. The worst of it is that these lice can travel about enough to get into the hair of perfectly clean people. They may also be caught from wearing the hats or caps of those who have lice on their heads. It is unsafe even to hang one's hat or wraps near those of a person who has lice.

Clean, well-combed, healthy looking hair is one of the greatest attractions we can have. On the other hand, hair that is greasy, dirty, or which has a bad smell is never attractive, to say the least. One's personal habits and cleanliness are constantly judged by the appearance of his hair.

CARE OF THE HAIR

Bad habits to avoid about the hair.—1. Some boys allow their hair to become rough, tousled, and unruly from lack of proper brushing. This shows them to be careless about their person and not to have very good taste.

2. Girls sometimes let their hair become greasy, stringy and snarly because they do not take time to wash it. No one whose hair is in this condition is very attractive.

3. Some persons form the habit of scratching the head. If the head itches, the scalp either needs better care and attention, or else head lice are troubling. In either case, the difficulty should be remedied and we should not attract unfavorable attention to ourselves.

4. Putting oil on the hair. Nature supplies enough oil from the roots of the hairs if we take good care of the hair. Oil put on the hair only makes it gummy and sticky.

Hair habits that will make one ready for "inspection."—1. Washing the hair thoroughly with soap and warm water twice a week. It is well to have certain days for this in order that it may not be forgotten.

2. Having one's own comb and brush and then neither borrowing nor lending. Especially ought one not to use combs and brushes found in hotels, railway wash-rooms or other public places.

3. Brushing the hair vigorously each night and morning and massaging the scalp once each day.
4. For boys to form the habit of keeping their hair clipped often enough so that it does not grow to look ragged and too long. For girls to have their hair always neatly fastened in some attractive way.

Health Problems

1. When Mary got home from school last night she told her mother she didn't like to sit next to Henry in class, because he was always scratching his head and it made her "creepy." What different causes might lead Henry to make himself unpleasant by scratching his head?
2. Dick wets his hair every time he combs it to make it "lie down" better. His mother tells him that wetting his hair so much only makes it more stiff and unruly, and that what he ought to do is to *wash* his head thoroughly twice a week and then *brush* his hair instead of wetting it. Do you think she is right about it?
3. Can you by looking around the school-room, pick out the girls and boys who take good care of their hair, and the ones who neglect their hair?
4. Make a list of six good "hair habits." How many of these habits have you formed?

CHAPTER XXV

KEEPING THE NAILS IN ORDER

Our finger-nails have three chief uses. They protect the ends of the fingers; they aid in picking up and holding small objects; and they add to the appearance of the fingers.

The nails, like the hair, are a part of the epidermis, or scarf skin, and therefore do not hurt nor bleed when we cut them. They grow from the root end, and no matter how they may be torn, bruised or injured, they will grow out again if the root has not suffered injury.

Certain fashionable people in India and China allow their finger-nails to grow out very long, sometimes as much as several inches. The nails are then kept carefully trimmed, polished, and even painted. Of course such long nails are in the way and their owner can not work, for the nails would be broken off. In fact a metal cap like a thimble is often worn over these long nails to keep them from breaking. We would think that such nails looked too much like claws and would not want them.

How to trim the nails.—Good taste and convenience both require that our nails shall be kept carefully trimmed. They should be left just long enough to project the least bit beyond the tip of the finger. Some trim their nails to a pointed shape, but this makes them more liable to break. The best way is to trim the nails in a curve to match the oval tips of the finger.

Sometimes the skin clings at the root of the nail as it grows out. This stretches the skin until it breaks, and fragments of it peel back. The breaking and peeling of the skin causes what we call *hang-nails*. Hang-nails not only become very sore, but also injure the looks of the fingers.

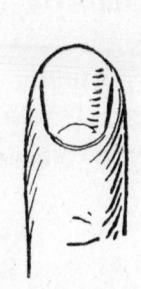

The one nail shows a rough and jagged edge where it has been broken or nibbled; the other shows careful care and trimming. Which would you rather have?

Curing hang-nails.

—Hang-nails will not form if the skin is not allowed to grow fast at the root of the nails. This can be prevented by pushing with the thumb against the skin at the back of the nail whenever the hands are washed. A soft wooden instrument may be used to push the skin back. The nails should never be scraped or scratched with any hard instrument, for this will only cause them to grow thick and unshapely.

KEEPING THE NAILS IN ORDER

One of the chief points in caring for the nails is to keep the dirt cleared from under their tips. The cleaning should never be done with a knife, scissors or any sharp instrument which may scratch and make the nail rough underneath. For this only makes a lodging place for the dirt and causes it to stick all the more readily.

Cleaning the nails.—The best instrument for cleaning under the finger-nails is a soft bit of wood sharpened just enough to go under the nails readily. Small wooden nail cleaners are sold in the shops for about one cent each, but one can easily make such an instrument for one's self.

If one's hands have become very much soiled, or the dirt has become caked under the nails or around their edges, it may be necessary to use a stiff brush in order to clean them well.

But whatever method we use, we should at least keep our nails clean. A black line under our nails is sure to tell tales on us, and let everybody know that we have not formed good habits of caring for our hands.

The dirt that lodges under the finger-nails also contains many different kinds of microbes. Some of these may bring us disease if they get into our mouths or on our food as we eat.

Accidents to the nails.—A young friend who lives neighbor to me recently made a mistake and struck his finger-nail in place of the nail he was driving into a board. Joe's finger-nail turned black and gave him a great deal of pain. He said it throbbed so that he could feel his heart beat in it.

The dark appearance of the nail was caused by the blood which flowed out from the small vessels which had been broken underneath the nail by the blow of the hammer. The throbbing was caused by the blood which was driven by his heart-beat against the torn and bruised nerves.

Joe's finger hurt him so that his mother took him to the doctor. The doctor bored a little hole through the nail and let the blood out. This relieved the pain. The doctor told Joe that if the blood was not let out it would harden underneath the nail and interfere with the growth of the new nail which Joe will have in place of the old one.

Caring for the toe-nails.—Toe-nails need as much care as finger-nails in order to keep them in good condition. Every time a bath is taken, the toe-nails should be cleaned under the tips and around the edges, and care should be given to see that they are not becoming too long.

Instead of cutting toe-nails in a circular form as is the case with finger-nails, they should be trimmed nearly square across. This is to keep them from growing under at the edges and causing *ingrowing toe-nails*.

KEEPING THE NAILS IN ORDER

Instruments for use on the nails.—The best way to trim nails is with a small pair of scissors or with a nail file. The file will do a better job than the scissors. A knife is not a proper instrument for trimming the nails, as we can not trim them with it in so true a shape, and there is always some danger of cutting where we do not intend to with the knife blade.

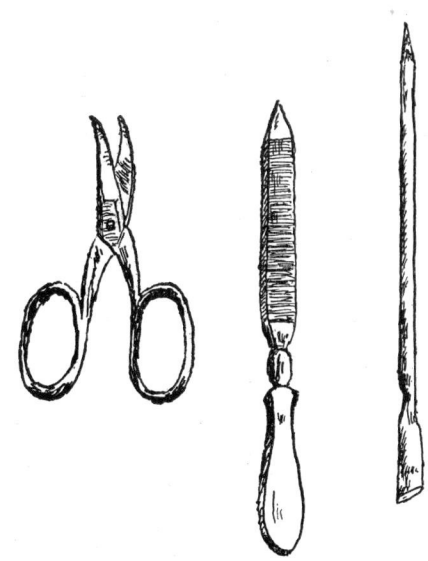

These three instruments, scissors, file, and a soft piece of wood sharpened to a dull point, cost but a few cents, and each member of the family should have his own set

Habits to avoid in caring for the nails.—1. Biting or nibbling the nails. This bad habit is not only disgusting to others, but it is also unsafe to take into one's mouth the microbes that lodge in the dirt under the nail tips.

2. Trimming the nails by pulling the tips off with the fingers. This leaves them rough and jagged and finally spoils their shape.
3. Scraping or filing the back of the nail. This

always causes the nail to grow thick and heavy and leaves the surface uneven.

4. Allowing dark lines of dirt to gather under the tips or around the edges of the nails.

Desirable nail habits to form.—1. Keeping the nails so carefully filed or trimmed that they are always ready for "inspection."

2. Using a soft wooden instrument each time we wash our hands to clean underneath and around the edges of the nails.

3. Pushing the skin back at the roots of the nails in the morning so that the little white crescent at the back will show clearly.

4. Taking as good care of our toe-nails as of our finger-nails.

Interesting things to do.—1. Show how to shape a piece of soft pine to make an instrument for cleaning under the nails.

2. Show how to push the skin back on the crescent of the nail to prevent hang-nails.

3. Show how to trim the finger-nails properly with small scissors.

4. Show how to trim the nails with a nail file.

5. Show how to trim the toe-nails to prevent in-growing nails.

CHAPTER XXVI

HOW TO HAVE GOOD EYES

Which do you think would be the most dreadful loss to one, to lose his sight, his hearing, his taste, or his smell?

I asked this question the other day of a group of boys and girls. They were to write down the answer on a piece of paper. When the slips of paper were collected, they all had the word "sight" written on them. I think the boys and girls were right about it. I can not imagine anything more dreadful than to be without sight. While the eye is well protected by being set back in a bony pocket, yet it is a very delicate organ and is easily injured. The eye may be injured by accidents, by diseases, or by improper use.

Guarding the eyes against accident.—John Lothrop Motley, the writer of histories, was made blind by a comrade throwing a bread-crust which struck him in one eye. The other eye became diseased by the inflammation and also lost its sight.

Two boys whom I know were playing together and one chased the other under the low hanging limbs of a tree. The one who was ahead caught a small branch with his hand and then let go of it. When the branch flew back a small twig struck the other boy in the eye and cut through the outer coating. This let out the liquid that fills the front of the eye, and made the eye blind. It had to be removed by the doctor, and my friend to-day wears a glass eye in place of his own.

Many accidents happen every year on the Fourth of July from the explosion of firecrackers, toy pistols and the like, which cause the loss of eyesight. One can not be too careful in guarding his eyes against accident, nor can he be too careful not to injure the eyes of another person.

The wrong way to sit when reading. The light should not strike the eye, but fall from behind or from the side on the page

Danger of overworking the eyes.—The eye is one of the hardest worked organs of the body. Our eyes were originally intended for out-of-door vision rather than for reading books. It is only a few hundred years since men have begun to read books in any numbers. In five minutes of reading on this page your eye makes about one thousand separate movements and focuses

HOW TO HAVE GOOD EYES

as many times with rifle aim precision upon the letters that you read.

Five minutes of such reading probably requires as much work of the eye as the energy expended in a whole day of distant seeing out-of-doors.

Rules for caring for the eyes.—If our eyes are to stand this hard work, we must give them the best of care. Some simple rules which we all need to follow are these:

1. We should not read while facing the light. Direct light tires the eye and weakens it. The best reading light comes from the side or over the shoulder, so that it falls on the page without any shadows. Good lighting from overhead may also be had. We should never sit facing a window nor reading lamp. Nor should we have strong electric lamps in our rooms without shades covering them.
2. We should not read in light that is too dim, for this strains the eyes unnecessarily. The light is too dim whenever we find it hard to see the print. We are sometimes careless when reading in the twilight as the light grows faint, and continue until it is far darker than is good for the eyes.
3. We should not read from blackboards that are shiny, so that they reflect the light into our eyes. Nor should we read from the blackboard when we are so far away that it is hard to read the letters.

HYGIENE AND HEALTH

4. The books we use should not have a very fine print. Trying to focus upon objects that are too small gives the eye extra work and strain.

5. It is easy to form the habit of reading with the page too near the eyes. We should notice the distance at which we can read best, and then be careful to keep our book at about that distance. For a book like the one you are reading you ought to read the print at about sixteen inches from the eyes, if your eyes are in good condition.

Reading on a train or in a street-car is hard on the eyes. This is because the jolting of the train causes the eye constantly to change its focus to keep track of the moving words. The muscles of the eye are soon tired, and may be seriously injured.

It pays to be good to our eyes.—We may think that our eyes are so strong that none of these things will hurt them. But we can never be sure, and we ought not to injure our eyes even if they are good. If we weaken our eyes we are sure to have to pay for it some day by being obliged to wear glasses, or being unable to see well. The doctors tell us that about one boy and girl out of four in the schools of the United States has serious eye trouble. Each of us ought to save our eyes in every way possible.

Diseases of the eye.—A disease called "pink-eye" is very frequently found in our schools. In pink-eye

HOW TO HAVE GOOD EYES

the eyes smart and are sensitive to the light, and the eyelids stick together at night. There is also usually some discharge out of the corners of the eye. The eyes look inflamed and red.

Pink-eye is commonly carried by means of towels, borrowed handkerchiefs, or by using wash-basins which others with bad eyes have used.

A still worse disease is that called *trachoma*. In this disease the eyes become inflamed, the lids swell and the surface of the eyeball becomes rough. The inner surfaces of the eyelids are covered with small granules, and are very painful.

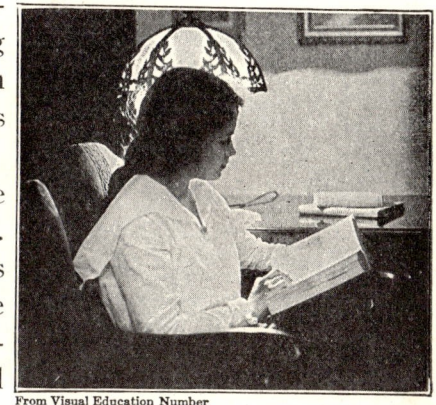

From Visual Education Number

The right way to sit when reading. The light does not strike the eye, but falls on the book

This disease is not so common as pink-eye, but it is much worse when one has it and may sometimes cause blindness. Trachoma is very contagious and can be contracted from the towels, basins, or handkerchiefs used by those who have the disease.

We should form the habit of keeping our hands away from our eyes, and especially never rubbing them when they smart or itch. We should not use any article of clothing that has been used by one who has sore eyes. We should not wash in the same basin with any one who has eye trouble.

Good habits in protecting our eyes.—1. Always sitting in such a position when reading that the light will come from overhead, the side, or behind us. It should never shine in the eyes.
2. Sitting up straight when we read instead of bending the head forward over our work. When we hang the head forward extra strain is put on the eyes.
3. Stopping reading when the eyes begin to smart or feel tired, or when we notice the light too dim to see easily.
4. Going to the doctor if our eyes become red, sore, or inflamed, or if they discharge and the lids stick together.

Bad habits about the eyes which we should avoid.—1. Rubbing the eyes with our fingers or with soiled handerchiefs, or towels which other people have used.
2. Looking at very bright lights or at the sun.
3. Reading while in bed or lying down so that the book is not held in a good position.

Interesting things to do.—1. Notice carefully whether the letters on this page look blurred. Whether they dance about. Whether they run

HOW TO HAVE GOOD EYES

together. If they do any of these things, you should have your eyes examined by the doctor.
2. Place your book flat against the wall in a good light. Then go exactly fifteen feet back and see whether you can easily read every one of the first line of letters at that distance. If not you should have your eyes examined. Do the same for the second line at ten feet.

R T V Z B D F H
(15 feet)

V Z Y A C E G L N P R T
(10 feet)

Health Problems

1. Are your eyes good: Can you read the print of this book easily at a distance of about sixteen inches from the eye? Do your eyes begin to smart after you have read for some time? Does your head ache from reading?
2. A boy who had eyes which looked inflamed and which were running somewhat at the corners, kept rubbing his eyes with his fingers, which were rather dirty. What reasons can you give why one should not rub his eyes with his fingers?

CHAPTER XXVII

CARE OF THE EARS

While some one is talking near by put your finger-tips into your ears and then try listening to the conversation. Does it not sound strange? Everything is blurred, and now and then there are words that you can not hear at all. You miss a great deal of what is said, and finally lose the meaning of the conversation.

Would it not be dreadful to have your ears like that all the time? Yet there are many children who have some kind of ear trouble that makes it impossible for them to hear any better than you can with your ears stopped up.

Many children have poor hearing.—Physicians who have carefully examined the ears of children in many schools tell us that nearly one-fifth of all the school children in the United States have some ear difficulty which makes them hard of hearing.

In school one who is hard of hearing does not hear all the teacher says about the lesson. He may miss the assignment or some important explanation. He finds it hard to prepare his lesson and soon falls behind the class. Many such children are thought to be dull

CARE OF THE EARS

when the real trouble is not in the brain at all, but in the ears.

The strange thing about poor hearing is that it may come upon us without our knowing it. Unless our hearing becomes very bad, it may grow dull without our realizing that other people hear better than we do.

How to detect poor hearing.—If one seems to have trouble to hear what the teacher is saying in school, it is well to notice whether others round about seem to be hearing clearly. If so, it is possible that he has dullness of hearing that should receive attention from the doctor.

Another way to test the hearing is by listening to the tick of a watch. Seat yourself in a chair and close your eyes. Have some one take a watch and hold it close enough to your ear until you can clearly hear it tick. Then have him move the watch slowly away until it reaches the point where you can no longer hear it. Do this several times, and measure carefully to find out the greatest distance at which you hear the tick.

Try this for both ears in the same way. Then have several others try it. If most of your classmates can hear the watch considerably farther away than you can, it means that your hearing has some difficulty that needs attention from the doctor.

Earache and poor hearing.—Still another sign of troublesome ears is to have the earache. This does not mean that every one whose ears may sometimes ache has dullness of hearing. But the hearing is nearly always affected if one has earache very much. Sometimes the ear runs pus, or matter, which has gathered inside. Running ears show disease that the doctor should remedy. They many times lead to deafness.

Most of the ear troubles that children have can be cured by the doctor if taken to him in time. Any one who finds that his hearing is somewhat dull, or who has earache, or a discharge from the ear should therefore go to the doctor. This may save deafness later in life, and it will surely make one able to learn faster and better while he is in school.

How the ear is made.—The ear is a very remarkable part of the body. If you will have a friend stand with his ear turned toward a bright light, and then with your finger pull forward the projection just at the front of the ear, you can look down a small, round canal that leads straight into the head. The canal is nearly one inch long. At the end of this canal you will see a little membrane stretched across like the head of a drum.

Just inside this membrane there is a little chamber or cavity across which hang in a row three tiny little bones that are tied the one to the other. These bones lead on in to a still smaller cavity hollowed out of the bone of the skull. It is in this small inner chamber that the hearing is really done.

CARE OF THE EARS

From the cavity just back of the drum-head there is a small tube that leads to the back part of the mouth. Sometimes the germs of sore throat or tonsillitis succeed in getting up this tube into the ear. It is these germs that give us earache and cause the trouble which

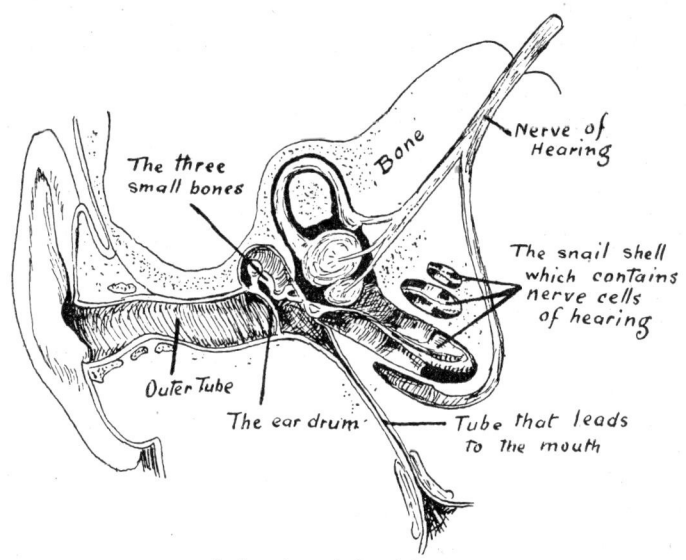

A drawing of the right ear

results in the discharge of pus from the ear. This is the reason why we often have earache along with bad colds or sore throat.

How we hear.—If you throw a stone into a pond of water you see the waves ripple out from the spot where the stone dropped. When I clap my hands together I make waves in the air just like those in the water where the stone strikes it. These waves in the air beat on the drum-head at the end of the canal and make it vibrate back and forth. The little bones carry the sound waves across to the ear inside.

A small friend of mine was playing on his drum recently and struck it so hard that he broke the membrane and ruined the drum. The drum of your ear is much more sensitive than the membrane on a drum-head. Sometimes a sudden blow on the ear will drive a rush of air against the ear-drum and cause it to break. This may injure the hearing in that ear.

Keeping the ears from injury.—You may have seen people pick at their ears with matches, hair-pins, toothpicks, or other sharp things. This is always dangerous. For if we even touch the drum we are likely to injure it. And without this drum-head we are deaf.

A very distinguished man whom I know has but one ear that hears. When he was a boy he was one day picking at his ear with his lead pencil, when some one passed him and jogged his elbow. This pushed the point of the pencil against the ear-drum and destroyed it.

A kind of wax naturally forms in the little canal that leads in to the drum-head. Ordinarily this wax comes out of its own accord, but sometimes forms in lumps. When it gathers in this way it should not be

CARE OF THE EARS

picked out. If we will drop into the ear a few drops of sweet oil or olive oil, this will loosen the wax so that it will come out without trouble.

Points to remember about our hearing.—

1. We may become hard of hearing without knowing it. If we have trouble to hear what people are saying we should have our ears tested. The doctor can do this in a few minutes, and with no pain or trouble to you.
2. Ear trouble and deafness often come from tonsillitis, adenoids, measles or scarlet fever. If our ears ache or run pus we are in danger of becoming deaf if they are not cured.
3. Most ear troubles can be cured if taken to the doctor in time. A stitch in time saves nine!
4. The ear should always be treated well. It should never be boxed nor pulled, nor should it ever be picked or the wax removed with any hard instrument.

Health Problems

1. Robert often misses hearing what the teacher says, although the rest of the class easily hear her. What two possible explanations are there of Robert's failure to hear the teacher?
2. Give rules for taking care of the ear. Do you follow these rules yourself?
3. Are you a good Health Crusader?

CHAPTER XXVIII

BETTER NOT—TOBACCO

The American Indians played one bad trick on the white people who drove them from their hunting grounds. The Indians taught their white neighbors to use tobacco. This was about the middle of the sixteenth century. The use of tobacco has spread until it is now known almost all over the world.

Rabbits and cigarettes.—In order to test the effects of cigarette smoke, a Russian scientist invented a piece of apparatus by which he could compel rabbits to breathe the smoke of cigarettes. In this way he had his rabbits smoke a number of cigarettes daily. Some of them died within a month, but others seemed to get used to the smoke, so that it did not appear to injure them. When these smoking rabbits were killed at the end of five months, however, it was found that their blood-vessels were diseased, and that their hearts did not act right. These effects were caused by certain poisons in the tobacco. So the cigarettes killed some and injured all.

Another doctor took one of these tobacco poisons, nicotine, and, parting the fur of a healthy rabbit, placed one large drop on the skin. The poison soaked through the skin into the blood and in a little time the rabbit sickened and died. He then tried putting two drops of nicotine on the tongue of a dog, and the same amount on the tongue of a cat. Both the dog and the cat died from the effects of the poison.

All tobacco contains a harmful poison.—The reason that smoking or chewing tobacco does not kill men is because they do not get all of the poison in this way. Much of it goes off in the smoke of the cigar, cigarette, or pipe. When the tobacco is chewed much of the poison is spit from the mouth.

Nevertheless the poisons from tobacco, whether it is chewed or smoked, do affect the heart and blood-vessels. Cigarette smoking is always found to increase the rate of the heart beat, thereby making it work harder than it otherwise would need to work. Careful experiments made upon soldiers showed that the smoking of a few cigarettes increased the pulse rate from six to nine beats a minute.

The smoker is usually short of breath. He lacks endurance. This is the chief reason why athletic coaches will not allow the men on their teams to smoke while they are in training. One can not help but wonder whether if tobacco is bad for an athlete, it is not bad for everybody.

Effects of smoking.—Dr. Bush in a series of tests upon fifteen different men found that immediately after smoking, these students showed a loss of more than ten per cent. in mental power. The loss was greatest when they smoked cigarettes.

Probably there is no man who uses tobacco but would be better off without it. Certainly there is no boy who uses tobacco but who injures his heart, clouds his mind, and hurts his chances for success.

The tobacco habit hurts one's business chances.—Great business concerns have come to learn that boys who smoke are not so trustworthy and not so efficient as those who do not. Many of the largest and most successful banks, stores and factories will not now employ boys who smoke cigarettes. If one is sure to injure his health, decrease his brain power, and shut himself from the best business chances by the use of tobacco, it would seem good sense to let it alone.

Tobacco using is not a very cleanly habit. Chewing tobacco is perhaps the worst, since it results in spitting in a filthy and disgusting way. Smoking is but little better, however, and one's breath, teeth, and mouth always show the unpleasant effects of tobacco.

The cost of tobacco.—Even the cost of tobacco is one important reason against its use. The person who smokes but one ten-cent cigar a day will spend $36.50 a year for his tobacco. If he smokes three cigars a day, his tobacco bill will be more than $100.00 a year.

BETTER NOT—TOBACCO

Surely there are many ways in which one could better spend his money than in burning it up in smoke which constantly harms him in place of doing him good.

Facts worth remembering about tobacco.—

1. Tobacco never helps a boy get or hold a job. It keeps many boys from securing the best jobs.
2. The use of tobacco, especially cigarettes, never fails to interfere with our growth and strength. It always dulls the mind and checks our development.
3. Money spent for tobacco is worse than wasted, for what we buy with it is sure in the end to do us harm. It never does us good.

Health Problems

1. It has been found that boys who use tobacco do not do so well in athletics as boys who do not use it. Which do you think a good, live boy should choose, cigarettes or the strength and skill that make him a good athlete?
2. By comparing the school grades of boys who use tobacco with boys who do not use it, it is shown that the tobacco users do not do as good work as the non-users. What would you say is the wise choice for a boy to make?
3. How many reasons can you give why a boy should not use tobacco? How many reasons why he should?

CHAPTER XXIX

BETTER NOT—ALCOHOL

Alcohol has recently been having a hard time of it. When the great war broke out in Europe in 1914, one of the first things each of the nations did was to forbid or limit the use of strong drink.

Russia banished vodka. France forbade absinthe. England limited the amount of beer and other drinks that could be bought. The United States passed laws against the manufacture and sale of certain liquors, and finally added an amendment to the Constitution which forbids the manufacture and sale of all alcoholic drinks.

Alcoholic drink always an enemy.—Action was taken against alcohol by the different nations because each one knew it must put forth its full strength in order to do its part in the war. Each nation knew that strong drink always injures and weakens the u

For centuries alcohol has deceived men and ma e them love to drink. The man who is intoxicated imagines that he is having a good time; he feels very strong, wise, and powerful. He does not know that he is really silly and stupid, and an object of pity.

BETTER NOT—ALCOHOL

Scientists have recently carefully measured the strength, endurance, and mental power of men who have not had alcohol, and then measured the same men after they had been given whisky or beer or wine to drink. In every case it has been found that alcohol decreases one's strength. It weakens his endurance. It confuses his mind so that he is less able to think.

Growth and ability injured by alcohol.—Even cats, dogs, chickens and guinea pigs which have been given alcohol show the effects. They fail to grow full size. They are dull mentally and can not learn. They do not live as long as they otherwise would. In fact, they are poor specimens of animals, just as men who become drinkers are poor specimens of men.

So sure is alcohol to steal away one's brain and lower his strength that railroads, factories, business houses, and other employers now quite generally refuse to hire men who drink.

Alcohol never helps in the end.—It used to be thought that wine and beer contained certain foods that were good for people, especially for the weak or the sick. It is now known that those who use alcohol are much more likely to take disease and die than those who have never used it. Many people think that a drink of whisky will enable one to stand severe cold. It has been clearly shown, however, that men who drink alcohol in any form are unable to stand exposure to either cold or heat as well as those who do not use it.

Alcohol is always an enemy and never a friend. Its use easily grows into a habit that men find impossible to break. It makes those who use it cruel and dishonest. It causes many crimes. It fills our jails and prisons.

When saloons were in existence in this country, more money was spent on alcohol in the United States in a year than is expended for the running of our public schools. Yet it shortens the lives of those who use it, robs them of their strength and manhood, ruins their careers, and causes much sorrow and distress to others.

No form of strong drink is safe.—There is no form of alcoholic drink that is wise or safe. A drink of beer is not so bad as a drink of whisky, only because it contains less alcohol. But more beer is drunk than whisky, so perhaps it really does more harm in the end. Wines are also less strong than whisky. But there is no drink that contains alcohol which is not foolish and harmful.

Interesting things to do in studying about alcohol.—1. Find out whether the law against the use of alcohol is well obeyed in your city. In your state.

2. Each member of the class might ask some successful banker, doctor, lawyer, or other business man what he thinks about the use of alcohol. Ask these men whether they would want to employ any one who drinks.

CHAPTER XXX

WHEN ACCIDENTS HAPPEN

Probably not many of the boys and girls who study this book have had really bad accidents, or have been hurt severely.

But suppose each of you stop now and make a list of all of the cuts, bruises, sprains, punctures of the skin, burns, or other kinds of small hurts you can remember having had in the past year. Very likely you find it quite a list, and one never knows when a still more serious accident or hurt may come.

What to do.—There are two things necessary if we are to do the right thing when we have an accident. First, we must *know what to do*. Second, we must *keep a cool head*.

Almost any small wound will heal readily if we make certain of two things about it:

1. Wounds must be cleaned of any splinters, bits of gravel, dirt or any other such substance that may have got in.
2. Bacteria must be kept out of wounds, or pus will form and the wound be slower in healing.

HYGIENE AND HEALTH

Medicines that cleanse wounds.—Whenever a wound runs pus we may know that the bacteria have got in and are at work. In order to clean wounds from bacteria, the surgeons wash them with what they call an *antiseptic*. This may be *iodine*, *hydrogen peroxide*, or any other one of several medicines.

This shows where the large artery of the neck and arm runs

One of the most common forms of wounds is cuts. If the cut is severe, there is usually a good deal of bleeding. If the blood spurts from the wound strongly, it means that an artery is cut, while if it flows steadily a vein is cut. Arteries carry the blood *from* the heart; veins carry blood back *to* the heart. If the flow is strong we should call the doctor to stop the bleeding and dress the wound.

Stopping bleeding from a cut by tying handkerchief loosely around the arm and then twisting it tight with a stick

How to stop bleeding.—But we shall need to do something immediately to stop the bleeding before the doctor

WHEN ACCIDENTS HAPPEN

comes. Unless the cut is very deep and the bleeding rapid, it can usually be stopped by pressing the fingers tightly over the cut. If this does not check the flow of blood, a handkerchief should be tied just

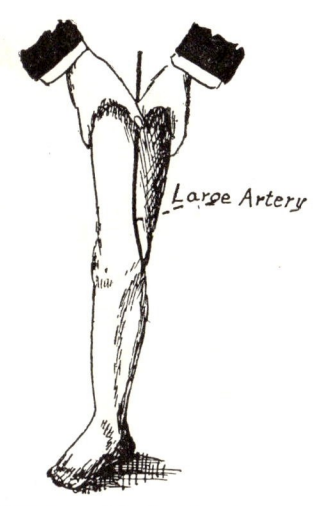

Pressure with the thumbs over the large artery of the leg will check bleeding while a bandage is being prepared. The pressure must be *above* the cut

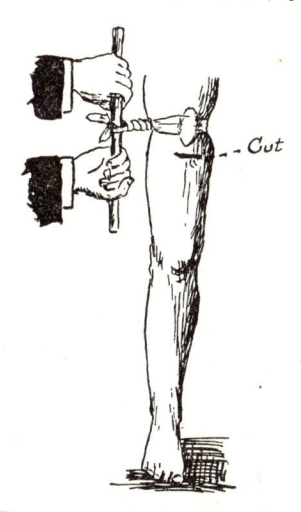

To stop severe bleeding from the large artery of the leg, a handkerchief should be tied loosely around the leg above the cut, a piece of stick placed over the artery, and the handkerchief then twisted tight

above the cut and then twisted tight with a stick until the bleeding stops.

The doctor will wash the cut out with an antiseptic, and then if the wound gaps open, pull the edges together either with tape or with stitches. If the cut is not severe enough to call the doctor, we can cleanse the cut and apply the tape ourselves.

Treating bruises. — Bruises are sometimes as serious as cuts and need to be treated as carefully. If the skin has been broken through, the bruised place should be carefully washed with an antiseptic and all of the dirt and foreign substances carefully removed. A piece of absorbent cotton wrung out of the antiseptic solution may then be laid over the bruised place and a bandage put over the whole. Cold cloths are sometimes applied to bruised places in order to keep the soreness and swelling down.

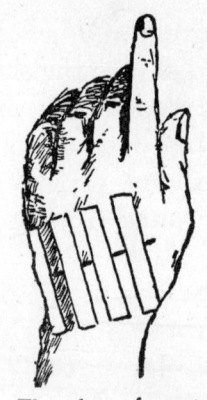

The edges of a cut may be held together by strips of adhesive tape

Punctured wounds. —Puncture wounds are often more dangerous than either cuts or bruises. We may step on a rusty nail and not feel the hurt greatly at the time. It is entirely certain, however, that a

Adhesive plaster applied to cuts on the face. This treatment will aid in the healing and will help prevent scars

great number of bacteria are carried by the point of the nail into the skin. Since the punctured wound does not bleed much, the bacteria are not washed out by the blood as many of them are in a flowing cut wound. Blood poisoning, or even lock-jaw, often follows a wound from a dirty nail.

If the skin has been punctured by a clean nail or a bright needle or pin, there is less danger. Any punctured wound should be squeezed immediately, however, to force the blood out if possible. Iodine or alcohol should be spread freely over the punctured place and even poked down into the hole with the point of a clean toothpick.

Taking care of a sprain.—Sprains are often very troublesome hurts. Sprains are caused by the tearing or pulling loose of little bands called ligaments, which hold the bones together at the joints. If the sprain is severe, the smaller blood-vessels are broken and the blood gathers about the sprained part. This causes it to swell and also helps to increase the pain.

The sprained part should immediately be plunged into cold water, which will help keep the swelling down and stop the pain. This may be changed after a time to very hot water, which will have the same effect. If the sprain is severe enough to cause much pain, the joint may require bandaging. In applying the bandage care must be taken to make it draw tightly over the softer portions around the joint, for these are the places around the joint, for these are the places where the blood will settle and the swelling be most severe.

If the sprain is slight, it is best to exercise the sprained part lightly to keep it from getting stiff. If it is too severe it may be necessary to rest the joint for a number of days.

Burns.—When burns occur, the very first thing to do is to shut the air from the burned part. This can be done by plunging the burned place into cold water. If, however, a large portion of the body has been burned, as from the clothing taking fire, then it is better to put the person, clothing and all into warm water, as in a bath-tub.

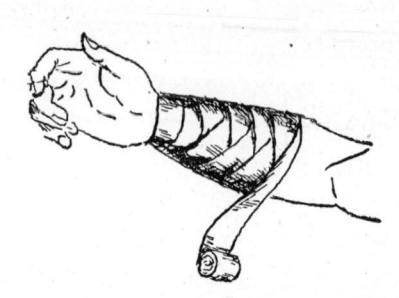

One way of bandaging for a sprain

If the burn is severe the doctor will, of course, be called and will tell what to do next. The burn should be kept from the air, however, until the doctor has arrived. This will save pain and will make it easier to treat the burn afterward.

It is a mistake to put anything on burns that will stick to them and make pain and trouble in getting the substance off.

If the skin is only red and not blistered or broken through, the burn may be covered with a clean cloth that has been soaked in water in which ordinary cooking soda has been dissolved. This will serve to keep the air from the burned place, and will lessen the pain. If the skin is blistered or broken through, however, salad oil, castor oil, glycerine, vaseline or fresh lard without salt can be put on the burned place till the doctor comes.

When the skin blisters from a burn, it should be dressed with oil, and then not disturbed for about twenty-four hours. At the end of this time the liquid must be let from the blister. This can best be done by snipping through the top of the blister with sharp scissors.

Frost-bites.—If we frost the nose, ears, fingers, or any other part of the body, it immediately turns white because the blood has stopped flowing through. The great secret of caring for a frost-bitten part is to thaw it out gradually. A handful of snow or plunging the frozen part into a basin of cold water is far better than to thaw it out in warm water or in the heat of the fire. Thawing a frost-bitten part with warm water or fire heat not only causes intense pain, but makes the place more sore afterward.

Chilblains are caused by poor circulation of the blood in the feet. This is usually brought about by cold feet, or by tight shoes worn in the winter-time. Going with wet feet also tends to cause chilblains. Chilblains cause the feet to become very sore and to itch badly.

To cure chilblains it is necessary to keep the circulation of the feet good. This can be done by keeping the feet warm, wearing shoes that do not bind, and by rubbing the feet, especially at night. Healing ointments may also be rubbed on the sore places.

Dog bites.—Everybody loves a good dog, and a healthy dog often makes a splendid playfellow. Occasionally a dog or cat bites some one; this always causes much anxiety because the bite of an animal may prove fatal if germs of the disease called *rabies,* or *hydrophobia,* are present in the animal's mouth at the time of the injury. Nothing applied to the wound will have any effect in preventing rabies but the wound should be dressed for comfort and cleanliness.

If the dog was being teased it is quite probable that this caused his action rather than the disease called rabies; in this case he should be shut up where he can be watched; if he begins to act strangely or appears to be "running mad" he should be killed and the head sent to the State Board of Health Laboratory for examination.

If the laboratory reports that the animal had rabies "Pasteur treatment" should be administered to the injured person at once. This will be sent upon request from the State Laboratory or from your nearest Branch Laboratory to be administered by your local physician or health officer.

WHEN ACCIDENTS HAPPEN

In this way the contraction of rabies or hydrophobia can nearly always be prevented, but it is well to avoid danger by keeping a safe distance from strange dogs and cats and especially from animals which act strangely.

Interesting things to do.—1. Play that you have cut your wrist and that it is bleeding. Put an ink mark on the skin to represent the cut. Now show how to hold the cut shut with the fingers of your other hand so it will not bleed.
2. Play one of the class has cut his arm badly just above the elbow. Show how to put a handkerchief around the arm and then twist it tight with a stick to stop the bleeding.
3. Show how to bathe and bandage an ankle for a bad sprain.
4. Show how to treat frost-bitten fingers, nose or ears.
5. Find out where your nearest State Laboratory is located. Write your State Board of Health for additional information about rabies.
6. Play that a burn has blistered the back of your hand. Show just what to do in caring for it.
7. Make a Health Crusader report showing the good health habits you have formed while studying this book.

CHAPTER XXXI

GOOD HEALTH GAMES*

This lesson is not to be learned and recited upon as are most lessons of the text. It is made up of interesting things to do from time to time as your teacher may direct. In it are some games, exercises and drills which you are sure to like. Their purpose is to rest you after you have been studying, to give you fun, and to help you to grow straight and strong.

You should study the directions for each game or exercise until you are sure you understand just what movements are required. When the teacher gives the directions each one must listen carefully so that no mistakes shall be made when the game begins. Much of the success and fun will depend on how quickly you think and understand, and how skilfully you carry out the directions.

In some of these games, as for example the two immediately following, we *imagine* that we are somewhere else or that we are somebody else and then do the things

---

*The games and exercises of this chapter are largely borrowed or adapted from the Michigan and the California State Manuals of Physical Training. Write to State Board of Health or State Tuberculosis Association for additional material.

GOOD HEALTH GAMES

that are required of us. The teacher or the book tells us what to do, our imagination helping all the while.

When the games are played indoors *the windows should be open!*

Making Christmas toys.—1. *Jack in the Box.* At a signal from the teacher pupils all *stand* in correct position, on both feet, body straight, arms at sides, head

Outdoor fun and frolic go with good nature and health

up, chin in. The teacher makes a downward motion with the hand as if closing a box; all quickly *bend knees* until almost sitting on heels. The teacher suddenly raises her hand and all *spring up* to a standing position.

2. *Jumping Jacks.* At a signal from the teacher all stand (correct positions). The teacher makes a motion as if pulling a string. Pupils *jump* into the air with feet apart, bringing them together again as they land. The arms are to be brought *up* to a level with the shoulders and *down* again with each jump.

Playing in the snow.—At a signal from the teacher pupils "get sleepy"—*heads laid on arms* resting on desks, *body relaxed*. (Keep this position for one full minute.) At second signal all "wake up"—*sit straight, stretch arms, yawn*. The teacher suggests a play in the snow to liven us up. At a signal all take correct *standing* position in aisle. At signal, "Boots," pull on rubber boots, first right, then left. At, "Caps," pull cap over ears (keep elbows out and back). It is so very cold that the teacher will give the signal, "Warm fingers." Pupils fling arms across chest slapping opposite shoulders. At signal, "Snowball," stoop low and *pick up* handful of snow. Make snowball while standing erect. *Throw snowball* at some object in the room. Repeat and throw with left arm. At signal, "Snow drifts," *walk* (without leaving place) through deep drift with hands on hips, lifting feet and knees high with each step. At signal, "Run home," go through *motions of running* (in place), taking long, *deep breaths* of pure air. The arms are to be raised straight from sides to shoulder height as breath is taken in, and lowered as it goes out.

Group games such as those which follow are suitable for playing in the school room for rest exercises and fun. Each player must be careful not to injure property or be unnecessarily noisy and boisterous.

Night before Christmas.—The players form in a circle and each is given the name of something connected with the story of Santa Claus, as sled, chimney, bells, mittens, fur coat, stockings, candy, etc. One player is chosen to be "it" and stands in the center while he tells a Christmas story in which he uses now and then the words given the players as names. Whenever he mentions the name of any of these things the one who has this name must turn completely around. If Santa Claus is mentioned, *all* must turn around. If the one who is "it" can tag any player before he has turned around, the one tagged must be "it" and go on with the story. The game may be made more difficult by having the players sit.

Tag the wall relay.—Two or more complete rows of players are seated at their desks. At a signal from the teacher the players in the rear seats rise, run down the aisle, tag the wall and return to their seats. As soon as the first player is in his seat the one next ahead does the same, and so on until each player has had his turn. The line whose front player is seated first wins. The game may be changed to tagging the blackboard by having each player write upon it some word agreed upon, passing the chalk to the next runner as he takes his seat.

Ducks fly.—The players stand facing their leader. The leader may say, *"Horses run,"* himself at the same time starting to run *in place*. All must imitate the running. But if the leader should say *"Trees run,"* then the players do not imitate the leader's running. If a player makes a mistake and imitates the running when the wrong words are spoken, as, *"Trees run,"* then he must be "it" and carry on the game. Many other exercises may be used, as jump, fly, swim, breathe, throw, catch, whirl, etc. Whenever a player *fails to imitate* when he should, or *imitates when he should not* the score is counted against him.

Bean bag relay.—The players are seated, a bean bag on each front desk. At a signal from the teacher each front player takes the bag and tosses it up and back over

Start for run in place with knee upward

his head. The player behind him must *clap his hands* after bag is thrown and then catch it or pick it up and do the same with it. The rear player, on getting it, hops down the aisle to the front of the room and there executes some movement previously agreed upon (as bending to touch his toes with his fingers); while he is doing this all the other players move back one seat. When he has finished the movement the player from the rear takes the front seat and the play begins as at first. This continues until the player who was in the front seat reaches it again and puts the bag on the desk as in the beginning. The row accomplishing this first wins.

Fetch and carry relay.—A circle eighteen inches in diameter is drawn in front of each row of seats close to the front wall. Each pupil is given a bean bag. At a signal each front pupil runs forward, places his bag in the circle, and resumes his seat. His being seated is the signal for the next to do the same, and so on till all the bags are in the circle. The first row to finish wins, providing every bag is *in the circle*. The play may now be reversed. At the signal the last player goes and gets his bean bag and after he is seated he touches the one in front of him as a signal to go. In this way all the bags are brought back to the seats, the row whose last player is seated first being the winner.

School room basket ball.—A basket is placed in the front seat of the second row from each side of the room. Draw a throwing line on the floor twenty feet from each basket. Choose four captains and have these captains choose teams, choosing in turn. The teams are to stand behind their throwing lines, each team having a ball. Captains stand beyond the baskets, two captains at the same basket. Each captain passes the ball in turn to his player and they throw for the basket. The team throwing the most baskets in a round wins *one point;* the first to get *five points* wins the contest.

In the exercises which follow the teacher will give the direction describing exactly what each one is to do. Immediately at the end of the description of the movement she will give the *command*, such as BEGIN! or ONE! or TWO!, etc. Each member of the class is to listen carefully so as to know what is to be done, and then at the *command*, act instantly. Be sure not to act ahead of the signal, nor, on the other hand, to be slow about obeying the command.

For example, suppose the class are all standing in correct position ready for a "warming up" exercise. The teacher will say:

On right foot, BEGIN! (At word BEGIN! you are to stand on the right foot.)

Hopping eight times on right foot, BEGIN! (At word BEGIN! you are to start hopping, *in place;* stop with the eighth hop.)

GOOD HEALTH GAMES 203

Warming up exercise.—Hands on hips, PLACE. (Body erect, head up.)

(1) Feet apart, JUMP! (Jump in air, landing with feet apart.)

A good way to spend a vacation

(2) Feet together, JUMP! (Back to position.)
In rhythm, BEGIN! (Continue jumping, bringing feet apart and then together as teacher counts 1, 2 until the command, POSITION!)

Stretching exercise.—(Repeat three times.) Bend knees deeply, reaching finger tips to floor, ONE! (Be sure to wait for signal ONE, then act promptly.)

Stretch knees and raise arms to vertical, TWO! (Arms stretched high above head.)

Lower arms to side horizontal, palms up, THREE! (Arms extended outward to right and left on level with shoulder.)

Position, FOUR! (Back to correct standing position.)

The "swing" drill.—Left foot forward, PLACE. (Left heel eight to twelve inches ahead of right toe.)

(1) Raise arms upward, forward with weight all thrown on forward foot, ONE! (Be sure to wait for the signal ONE.)

(2) Return, TWO! (Throw weight to other foot, but keep the feet in place.)

Also repeat in rhythm eight times, BEGIN! (The teacher counts 1, 2 for the changes.)

POSITION! (Back to standing position. Repeat with right foot forward.)

GOOD HEALTH GAMES 205

Chopping wood.—Feet apart, JUMP: (As in the warming up exercise).

Ax over right shoulder, PLACE! (Swing an imaginary ax above right shoulder as if ready for a stroke.)

(1) Swing ax downward and bend body forward, ONE! (Strike with ax as if chopping a tree.)

(2) Raise body and return ax above shoulder, TWO! (Ready for another stroke.)

Also in rhythm four times, BEGIN! (That is, repeat chopping blows four times, then come to position.)

Repeat from left shoulder.

Prancing of horses.—Hands on hips place and feet, CLOSE! (At CLOSE the hands are on hips, thumbs forward, feet close together, body in correct standing position.)

Left knee upward, BEND! (Lifting it high.)

Prancing in rhythm, ten times, BEGIN! (As if running, in place, knees lifting high.)

Arms and feet, POSITION! (Correct standing position.)

206 HYGIENE AND HEALTH

Deep breathing.—(Repeat from five to ten times.) Inhale with arms lifting sideward and heels rising, ONE! (Breathe in very slowly and deeply, beginning with ONE.)

Exhale as arms and heels return, Two! (Slowly and as completely as possible.)

An easy way to learn correct posture.

Climbing the ladder.—Raise left hand and left foot to rungs of ladder in act of climbing, ONE! (Wait for ONE.)

Position, TWO! (Be sure to hold first position until TWO is given.)

Repeat in rhyme eight times, BEGIN!

Also repeat with right hand and foot.

Pumping a bicycle tire.—Feet apart, JUMP. (Jump into air, landing with feet well apart.)

Imitate pumping, bending body forward and downward, ONE! (Bend well downward, pushing arms downward as if on bicycle pump at same time.)

Raise body, TWO! (Body erect, feet still apart.)

Also in rhythm, eight times, BEGIN! (Continue for eight strokes, then erect, feet still apart.)

Feet, POSITION! (Back to correct standing position.)

Blowing feathers.—(Repeat five to ten times.) Inhale with head moving backward, ONE! (Slowly, and remember that the more air you take in the more you will have to blow out.)

Blow hard, TWO! (As if blowing a feather from your lips high up in air, until your breath is all out.)

Perhaps your teacher may give you still other exercises and games, for there are many that we have not room to print in the text. Possibly you can even make up some new ones yourself. But whatever you do *make sure that you always play your games in pure, moving air.*

INDEX

Accidents, ch. on, 187
Adenoids, 92
Air, and breathing, 88, 135
    dry, and breathing, 99
    for the skin, 97
    living in pure, 95
    need of, 89
    open-air schools, 96
Alcohol, ch. on, 184
    effects of, 185
Bacteria, ch. on, 65
    and diseases, 69
    and food, 68, 72
Bathing, need of, 123
    after games, 137
    rules for, 122
Bleeding, stopping of, 188
Blood, the circulation of, 105
Breakfasts, right and wrong kinds, 52
    how to plan, 53
Breathing, experiments in, 88
    getting short of breath, 106
Bruises, how to treat, 190
Burns, treatment of, 192
Carbon dioxide, how produced, 90
    getting rid of, 90
Chest, expansion of, 94

Cigarettes, effects of, 186
Clothing, ch. on, 127
    cleanliness of, 131
    materials for, 129
    requirements of, 128
Colds, causes of, 120
    driving away, 121
Dandruff, 156
Dinners, how to plan, 54
Disease, bacteria and, 69
    flies and, 78
    mosquitoes and, 83
Dreams, 141
Ears, ch. on, 174
    aching, 175
    protection of, 178
    structure of, 176
Eating, experiments in, 51
    between meals, 61
    rules for, 59
Energy, coming from food, **34**
Eyes, ch. on, 167
    accidents to, 167
    care of, 169
    diseases of, 170
    overworking, 168
    tests for, 173

INDEX—Continued

Flies, ch. on, 77
   and disease, 78
   keeping out, 79
   preventing hatching, 79
   protecting food from, 78

Food, and bacteria, 68, 72
   necessary kinds of, 38, 41
   likes and dislikes for, 62
   why the body needs, 32
   kinds to be omitted, 57

Frost-bites, 193

Fruit, as a food, 45

Games, ch. on, 195

Gastric juice, 50

Growth, bodily, 33

Habit, ch. on, 1
   the forming of, 4
   friend-habits, 5
   enemy-habits, 6

Hair, ch. on, 155
   care of, 157
   insects in, 158

Health, ch. on, 16
   health "crusaders," 22
   health "chores," 26

Hearing, detecting poor, 175
   causes of poor, 177

Heart, the, ch. on, 104

Heat, from food, 36
   regulation of bodily, 116

Heredity, effect of on size, 26

Hygiene, exercises in, 14, 20, 21, 26, 30, 39, 47, 57, 63, 70, 76, 81, 87, 88, 93, 101, 108, 113, 115, 121, 126, 132, 134, 138, 143, 148, 153, 159, **165**, 172, 179, 183, 186, 194

"Inspection," school, 3
   class, 10
   personal, 10-15

Lunch, school, 57

Lungs, protecting the, 92
   size of, 91
   work of, 90

Meals, planning of, 49
   good cheer at, 50
   playing before and after, **136**

Meat, as a food, 44

Microbes, ch. on, 65
   and food, 68, 72
   where found, 65
   work of, 66

Mosquitoes, ch. on, 83
   and disease, 83
   getting rid of, 85

Nails, ch. on the, 161
   cleaning the, 163
   curing hang-nails, 162
   trimming the, 161
   toe, 164

Oxygen, in the body, 90, 106

Perspiration, 117, 119

Pores, 119

Posture, ch. on, 109
   harm from bad, 109
   sitting, 111
   sleeping, 115
   standing, 114

Ration, the balanced, 42

Record blank, health, 29

INDEX—Concluded

Rest, 139
Saliva, 50
Schools, open-air, 96
Size, at different ages, 17
    things that affect, 19
Skin, ch. on the, 116
    need of air for, 97
    cleanliness for, 122
    structure of, 118
    work of, 117
Sleep, ch. on, 139
    habits of, 140
    out-of-door sleeping, 142
    posture in, 115
Spine, curvature of, 112
Sprains, 191
Supper, how to plan the, 56

Sweat glands, 119
Teeth, the, ch. on, 144
    care of, 149
    crooked, 146
    dangers to, 153
    decayed, 147
Temperature, in rooms, 100
Tobacco, ch. on, 180
    poisons from, 181
    and success, 182
Vegetables, as a food, 45
Ventilation, rules for, 98
Water, as a food, 46
Wheat, as a food, 44
Wounds, care of, 187
    punctured, 191